Unfiltered

Editors:
Rick Shapiro and Tracy R. DeMarzo

'Sessions' Editor:
Robert Leach

Contact:
www.rickshapiro.tv

Management:
Tracy R. DeMarzo
TEAM SHAPIRO
rickshapiroupdates@gmail.com

Cover Art/Photography by:
Cat Gwynn: www.catgwynn.com

ISBN-13: 978-0692028285 (Custom)
ISBN-10: 0692028285

INTRODUCTION, from Tracy:

New pack of cigarettes.
He only smokes non-filters. The burn is more direct.
Tap. Tap. Tap… you have to pack them first.
"Where are the lighters?"
He always places them in the front pockets of his pants.
He smokes only *UNFILTERED* cigarettes.

When Rick and I first started working together in 2007, rather living together in 2007, he moved into my home with three Hefty bags full of papers. To anyone else, these shards of toilet paper, diner placemats and anything else that could be written upon might have seemed like garbage. I promised him I would never throw them out. To him these were fragments of performances, meals mentally devoured and his mind. These were the inner workings of Rick Shapiro—his essence. These fragments were the integrity of the comedian to his craft.

Throughout these past four years I have collected these slices of his mind, these written blurbs of thoughts and phrases; these examples of one-liners which were never one-liners. These lone words, sometimes circled, sometimes illegible (to even me) were excerpts; the tools that guided him, reminded him, and kept his long-form comedy prose handy the moment before he got on stage—but never used.

However this book does not contain that content. This book contains the items not brought on stage to his comedy fans. I remember thinking one day as I watched the pile of papers collect on his desk – which at that time was our kitchen table. "He writes a lot."

Throughout the first two years of our relationship I threw Rick out of our home repeatedly; every time, collecting his writings and placing them in a suitcase. I never threw out a word, a scrap, a toilet paper shard.

This book is those writings. The chapters are as follows:

1. Drafts found but never sent in hotmail
2. Seeking Approvals: Found in Hotmail and Sent to Adrian
3. 2005
4. 2006
5. 2007
6. MySpace Blogs
7. SESSIONS: 2011

You will see that there is a gap in the years between chapter 6 to chapter 7 (2007 to 2011). It was in September of 2007 that Rick was involved in a car accident. He incurred a head-injury which caused amnesia. His writing was placed at a stand-still, until 2008—at that time a great deal of new content was created. We are pleased to say that that the content developed in 2008 can be found on his new comedy CD/album CATALYST FOR CHANGE, which was taped in early 2009.

Although Rick continued to write (various other things and blogs), his focus changed and the content varied to what would be considered more of a 'screen-play' format—I guess Los Angeles would have that effect on a person. We hope to release that developing publication sometime in later 2012: *COP STORY.*

From 2009 into 2010, again, new content was developed and that was taped during the blizzard of 2010 in NY, at the Bowery Poetry Club. His desire for the city brought him back to pay homage to the town where has stand-up career had begun. The DVD, titled: JUSTICE will be released in 2012.

That leaves us with the present, or at least the present period of which this book of writings was coordinated. Rick and I started a Tuesday night event called *"Rick Shapiro's Spoken Word(s) night."* This was a night to encourage all people with a creative flare to come and read what they penned privately. The range of participants spun from comedians, actors, housewives to professional writers (and anything in between). It was at this event that two things happened. One, Rick started to read his poetry aloud and two we met Robert Leach, the creator and publisher of a publication called 'Stanley the Whale.'

Rob's interest in Rick flourished, and Rick's friendship with Rob developed. Soon enough Rob was over to the home that Rick and I shared; taping Rick's thoughts and transcribing them. This section represents Rick's some of Rick's creative activities in 2011.

Rob's intro to this section (SESSIONS) tells of this intimate time with Rick.

So to say that the past four years have been productive is an understatement. As Rick's Manager, I get to see this process on a daily basis. He is a creative force unlike anything I have ever witnessed. The black and white photos of his desk and walls provide you with an eagle eye view into the 'organized chaos' of his production state—for this we thank Cat Gwynn for capturing what one Agent referred to as "scary", and what I called home. Our home was a place for creativity. On the walls, on the floor – complete chaos to others. From my perspective, it was a compost of fertility to not be compromised by stringent rules of neatness.

When I first started working with Rick, I was told by a fellow Manager, that "my innocence of the industry (and of Rick Shapiro) was that of "a deer in the headlights."" (I had to look that cliché up). No, I was far from any mental state of *"high arousal caused by anxiety, fear, panic, surprise and/or confusion."* I thought quite the opposite. I saw this man as an under-exposed force of creativity. 'This is the coolest thing I have ever seen, a mixture of words and humor, a poet with comedy, a comic jazz singer,' I thought. I wanted to sit cross-legged and snap my fingers. He was smoking a non-filter cigarette on stage, and he was enraged about something, almost anything and it all made sense. Never had I heard word structure like this—Such emotional gravity and depth like that of which I heard never heard or seen before. His performance was more than a ticket to a comedy show, more than a typical audience moment, watching him was a journey, an experience.

What I saw on stage was electricity and passion and this changed my life. I found him to be unique in execution and integrity. A physical display of childhood-innocence mixed with a sexuality and fire. A range that of *GENUINE CURIOSITY* that many considered an anomaly. I was captivated and although I knew very little about the comedy industry or Rick for that matter, I knew this man was to be my greatest professional investment.

(by the way.. WE ARE NOT A COUPLE and we NEVER, EVER HAVE SEX)

From Rob

I remember my very first experience seeing Rick. It was at his Spoken Word night, then held at the incredible Café Muse on Santa Monica Blvd near Vine St. I'll admit to not being aware of his talents or history at that point in mid-2011 and so just seeing him didn't make me think one thing or another. I recall just sitting there quietly (as I'm wont to do) and seeing a bevy of creative and moderately eccentric individuals roam around chatting with one another. Rick stood out. Yes, part of it was due to his unique look but really it was his actions.

The first thing I remember him doing was wandering randomly over to the microphone and talking into it in a shaky mumble. I thought to myself, "Obviously a regular, he seems a little eccentric." I didn't know it was his show. I didn't know anything. All I thought was, "I wonder when the show's gonna start. I hope this guy clears the stage so we can get going."

I look back at those thoughts and smile.

About 1 hour later, when Rick did his first set, it instantly hit me that this guy was special. He wasn't just funny, he was poignant. Truly. I've seen talented individuals try to be poignant but Rick was that without effort, without faking it. Everything he said was layered, culturally relevant, personal, and genuine.

In short, I was blown away.

A couple weeks later, I was again blown away when Tracy approached me to help them work on this book. How could I possibly say no? And yet, I was constantly telling them they'd be better off without me. Well, shit happens for weird reasons and I'm truly thankful to god(s), the fates, random chance, the psychic network, or whatever it is that guides our destinies because it's been an amazing experience.

And I could tell you that it's been amazing because of Rick's genius, Tracy's managerial graces, the creative anarchy that resides in their apartment, but none of that would really be true. The fact is that it's been a tremendous experience because these are two incredibly good people. And they have an awesome dog, 99, who bears mentioning because she's a great dog and sports a Mohawk.

The fact of the matter is that good people are hard to come by. Really hard. Especially in Los Angeles where everybody drops their life to pursue their dream and generally lose a little bit of their humanity along the way. Both Rick and Tracy have had life experiences that sound so intense that they'd have literally killed off lesser persons. They are battle-hardened individuals who have taken their experiences and produced something beautiful. For Rick, it's his stand-up, the content of this book (and much much more to come), his acting, his generosity, and his passion. For Tracy, it's having ensured that the content of this book (and Rick's health) hasn't been lost, it's her absolute dedication, it's her love.

Oh, but what of my part? What role have I played in this title? Well, the last chapter of this book is called Sessions. An apt name. Over the course of about 3-4 months, I visited Rick and sat down with him and his work. At first, I just read and absorbed the literal suitcases filled with crumpled pages of all-caps no-punctuation type. It was brilliant but there was no way I could easily interpret them. So, I came up with a solution: I'd record Rick reading his pieces and then type out what he read, word for word.

As you go through Sessions, you'll see the evolution from me attempting to edit his typed word through to me generating scripts of even the interruptions we'd occasionally have during the readings. I decided to go that route simply because Rick is about fluidity. Rick is about the moment. And in the moment, there was always true beauty to be found.

For instance, I recorded one example of Rick performing Live at his spoken word night: at the infamous Sabor y Cultura café. It's a great place for getting some coffee and working on a script, apparently not a great place for spoken word. I've included the interruptions like the Cappuccino machine and patrons walking through the stage. I also include Rick chatting with a neighbor.

The best thing I've done here, however, is just having met Tracy and Rick. I haven't known Rick or Tracy long but I feel I **know** them. They don't have the barriers I'm used to or that I, myself, put up. I'm hopeful for both Rick's success and our continued friendship.

Rob Leach
Editor: Stanley the Whale website and magazine

Thanks, gratitude, dedication:

From Tracy:

The process of collecting these 'pieces' took us to our very last cent. The best example of how belief in the product/process kept both of us determined, is the day when the "PROOF" arrived. On the day that the 'proof' arrived at our home, and unbeknownst to Rick, I hadn't eaten for two days. The phone and internet were both scheduled to be shut off. We had an empty refrigerator and empty packs of cigarettes were rummaged through over and over again with hope of possibly finding the one last remaining smoke. There were prescriptions to be filled, people to be paid and we were hiding to avoid the landlord for fear of the dreaded 'eviction letter'... stress and tears started to set in. But 'hope and belief' held me/us through. It was then a knock at the door came and broke the tension of desperation. "You got a package," Rick told me. I knew what it was. What arrived was the book – the "PROOF," but rather, the physical proof that this mission, this drive would all be a reality very soon. We held it in our hands and a hope and belief were once again renewed.

Without the help of family, new friends and old, we never would have made it. People literally filled out refrigerator, helped us on credit, and drove us places without question. Friends from 15 years ago helped us—because they too believed. The generosity and humanity that I have discovered throughout this process (the past four-years, as well) is overwhelming. So with this, I thank the following people:

THANK YOU

- Mr. and Mrs. John and Irma DeMarzo (Mom and Dad).
- Adrian Nicole LeBlanc, Journalist, confident and friend
- Mark Katz, MD, cousin and friend
- David A. Pierce and all of his Law Group from PIERCE LAW GROUP, LLP, Rick's Lawyer and our friend
- Paul Provenza, Executive Producer and Creator: *SATARISTAS, ARISTOCRATS, GREEN ROOM WITH PAUL PROVENZA and so much more*
- Rob Leach: stanleythewhale.com
- Aaron Sterling, VLAD THE RETAILER, Team Shapiro's second home
- Jimmy Lee Wirt, Multi Media Artist Extraordinaire
- Scott Cosgrove, Designer
- John A. Scarcella: Former President, Sony Professional Solutions of America
- Alex Sauickie, Founder of Chloe's Causes

All of our friends, Rick's fans, the Facebook community, and anyone that has supported, believed, and consistently been 'there' for TEAM SHAPIRO

...and to Amy Lee of the DAILY PLANET and staff for your kindness and friendship. Not to mention your unending supply of *UNFILTERED* cigarettes.

Rick's opening poem.

Shut the Door on Hope

I rose out of the shit
Into a pile of stupid shit

I was a little boy on the street
They said I looked like Blackie
Child abused like you've never seen, Man.

Brother
Where were you for me?
Where was I for anyone, including me?
Into 18 years of death!
I was violently somnambulant

The nightmare avoided me and dreams kept trying to give to me...
I went down into the depths of me and came back as notoriety
I am what I pretend to be
A narcissist playing innocent
Silently abiding by the rules in AA

Though they said there were no rules and still say it, but AA can you have it both ways?

I fought for something that didn't exist
Friendship!

I gave up family and friends

Lost and lost again and I settle continuously for shit

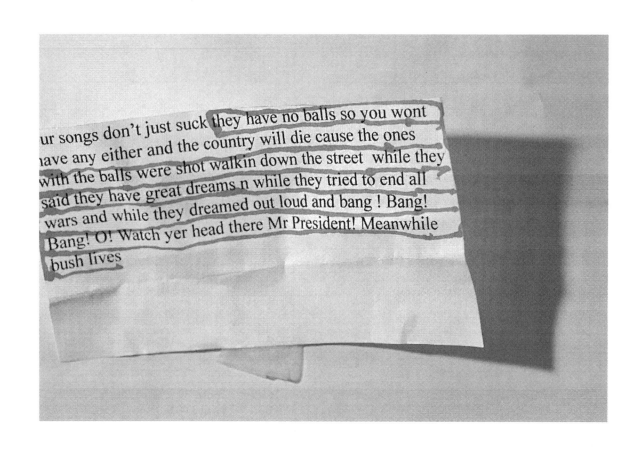

ur songs don't just suck they have no balls so you wont
have any either and the country will die cause the ones
with the balls were shot walkin down the street while they
said they have great dreams n while they tried to end all
wars and while they dreamed out loud and bang ! Bang!
Bang! O! Watch yer head there Mr President! Meanwhile
bush lives

Table of Contents

Drafts Found but Never Sent in Hotmail

Believe it

It's hard to believe.
I'm that guy who riffs, rambles, extols, demeans, exalts, hunts, rages, sweetifies, deifies,
and hates more... and loves wildly, and more... and paints — I mean and hurls and causes
and caused and causes and screws and screws and being taught to hold back.

And lives in the past.

Alone in Honolulu

When I try to talk to you
It's like being drunk
Alone in Honolulu!
Don't you love to rhyme?
Oh, it might be
Might sound like Jim Morrison time!

Hiroshima Style

Well, the roast beef is rare but I'd rather ATV with you in Cabo San Lucas
The last girl I was with there broke out in tears and wanted me to be a good Jew
Oh man, long story
Go ahead — roast beef
She thinks

Man you want the Cajun turkey and mustard?!
I mean just cause something's good don't make it right, Right, baby? And just cause
something's in good form or looks good or might even taste good don't make it any good at
all... You want mustard and we got 3 kinds, so take em'

And I'll put it on the bland, mild turkey that you always love and some of this and that and I'll
give ya the ass-eating-shit, sorry. The ass-kicking, turkey and smoked jack cheese baby...
Let's tear it up!

Well, you are right, I think.

If you don't like it I'll ride my bike onto, into a wall like jimmy dean; at least with the lust in my
eyes and your beauty well go out Hiroshima style!

Hey, there are others waiting. Can I help you?

No, it's ok!

(He leans to Rick) Yo! Dude! Make it. Not him. You always give me the real sandwich, not
his lil' bullshit-ness and yo, you gangster with that cheese! Yo!

Rick: I know man. It's like you wanna eat, not nibble and starve.

He runs and makes three sandwiches at once.

Manager: Make two!

Rick: Only two?

Manager: Only one. Really...

Whatchoo doin?

Ricky's down about the situation: Next, yeah you want the extra tuna, no charge and the bigger than life type beauty platter?
Ohhh, you already are that!

Cut to Rick at Ben & Jerry's and he's having ice cream.

Rick goes onto store and stutters...: Why do I always feel stupid? And why, why, why?

(Guy behind counter) Hey man. Hey! I saw you at that sandwich place. Your funny bro!

Rick goes home that night and sits and she watches TV and he smirks dumbly.
Look at her ass and nods semi-approvingly.
Why?
WHy?
WHY?
BOOM, BOOM, BOOM!

Can't Love

THE WHOLE WORLD WANTS TO HOLD BACK
I GET IT, I WAS THERE
I'VE BEEN THERE
THAT'S WHO I WAS SUPPOSED TO BE
HEY MAN, WHY NOT, IF THAT'S ALL YOU KNOW?
BUT WHO TRAINED US TO NOT HEAR THE RUMBLE?
THE EVENTUAL TEARING AWAY
THE THUNDER?
THE DEATH
THE DEATH KNELL
WHY WOULD WE WANT TO BE THE GUY WHO DOESN'T WANT TO HEAR IT?
THE GIRL WHO DOESN'T SAY 'OH YEAH RIGHT' AND 'YOU KNOW WHAT ELSE I
THINK I MEAN?'
COME ON MAN, A GUY WHO'S FASTER THAN YOU WERE TOLD?
OH, SLOW DOWN. WHY DIDN'T I JUST STAY? SLOWED DOWN
WHY, WHY OR WHY DIDN'T I GET IT RIGHT THE FUCK AWAY?
I KNOW MENTAL MEANDERINGS MEANT RAMBLINGS CLICHÉ, CLICHÉ, CLICHÉ.
DON'T LISTEN TO YOUR BRAIN!
THE ZEN BUDDHISTS ARE RIGHT
WHO CARES WHAT IF YOUR BRAIN IS MOTHERFUCKING TO THE RIGHT?
OPEN UP RICK, TALK ABOUT THE BUTTERFLIES THAT COME OUT THE MOTHS OF
CHILD ABUSE
TEAR IT OPEN ABOUT HOW YOU DON'T LOVE, CAN'T LOVE, WON'T LOVE
WHAT IS LOVE YOU CAN'T EVEN LOVE A SLICE ANYMORE OR DOGS?!
OH, YEAH BUT I LOVE IDEAS!
AND YOU'RE STILL AFRAID OF THEM
YOU'RE STILL LIVING IN A COUNTRY OF FUKKIN EFFICIENT FAGS AND EFFICIENT
COWARDS AND ENEMIES AND HETEROS – THE ONES WHO AREN'T AFRAID ARE
THE TRANNY'S, OR AS I LIKE TO CALL THEM THE MAVERICK SURREALISTS,
WALKING, TALKING VISIONARIES OF THE ABSTRACT

IGNORE THOSE WHO LOVE AND DON'T GO NEAR THOSE YOU COULD LOVE

DON'T GO NEAR LOVING YOURSELF, GET THE MONEY OR WAIT

 CALL SELF HATING, MISLED LIARS

YOU SEE THE RULES AS THEY WALK BY YOU; STIFFS STANDING AGAINST THE WALL

WONDERING HOW IT ALL HAPPENED

NOT KNOWING ITS CAUSE THEY BELIEVED AND WANTED YOU TO BELIEVE; MOTH

RIDDEN SLOGANS FARTIN' STRONGLY OUT OF WEAK DEAD SHEEP'S MOUTHS

YOU'RE IN THE DESERT

KEEP USING THE OLD PAYPHONE BY THE ABANDONED GAS STATION

BUT USE IT

THE SHEEP

I'LL TELL YA, THEY ARE THE RULERS

New Game!

Bjork.
Disney.
Be bold.
Bold pussy.
Right-wingers are as bold as they wanna be
And fake it
But if a
Lefty
Or radical is
Loud he must be... HE must be on drugs!
He must be angry!

Are you kidding?
They're in my face!
Hey *(whisper)!* Sleepy time, nicey, mousey, tea drinkin', cheesey.

THEY'RE IN YOUR FACE!

Hey, lil' FaceBook commenting
Sweetie, it's about the race!
The worlds too gay and let's redefine, re-awaken that!
I don't mean the real gay, the good gay, the alive gay, the gay that had balls for all balls can be, vibrating with gay
I'm talking about Grays Anatomy, GAY: The tighten you up, lighten you up, sick pup, never had the balls to try gay.

Reality show hosts.
Let's stay drunk.
That's what the fukkin commercials say
The government wants you too.
Titty play while they grab the money and go play!
You hear what I say? Cause, I'm hoping to get shot.
That's how I fukking play
This ain't on the internet
It's in your hearts!
It's your new game!
New game!

Sooo Human

True story.

You ever go into the zone and have to come back?

Tell your cop-buddy about why you won't carry a gun, because of all the hate and your fear of losing control...
Stretch that into a conversation with the criminal about how you are feeling his hate, and helping him get help about it.

I feel your hate buddy.
I mean what's your thing; the niggers the heebs the fagots the...
I mean the injustice or you being what, broke?
Or maybe ya did the right thing your whole life and ya realized the moneys right there, in the register.
To
NO
END!
To no end.
This town.
This country.
Aww hell... "this worrld!"

I mean what whatever happened to the real cowboys or any cowboys for that matter?
But you hold on to that one deeply intensely serious theatrically, utterly, funny reason, the world is fair!
I mean come on when you can see there is no justice at all ever
You, well, ya start to let things go and – well...
What's he doing man?
I didn't do nothing

Why?
Whyyy?
As self helpers would need to have me believe.

The safe tea drinkers.
The lavenders.
It's a balance.
Do something you are interested in.
Then do something you're not interested in, like get married.

If you see eroticism everywhere, everywhere the erotic hot steaming vibe is vibing your
vibing energy?
Sure, nice way to put it, your humanness
Your humanity, being the fact that you are human, soooo human!
You are only and always human.
Human!

I love that word!
So human.

Eatin' Ass: Realm into Eroticism

I'm going into Starbucks.
I see you n' I sit down n' draw you
N' I'm nuts
No, awake!
And I see yer ass crack or the book you read
and the thought in yer eyes.
And I want you and I'm seeing you look at me.

Your eyes your eyes your eyes your lips!
So wide awake!
Without you.
What lives in you!
I'm here.
The zone is me!
And then its room for milk…
What's yer name? Room for milk!
Coffee ain't a Christmas tree or fairy tale or the Christian coalition corporate merging.
Well it is that…
Or writhing passionate women and men of force and lovely unending desire
So it's just coffee man!
Relax or get wild, cause these people here are amazing.
Don't ruin it by ordering coffee and responding like coffee's a fairy tale,
> *'I'll have the cinnamon praline, frothy, dreams come true, auburn evening, summer,*
> *fantasy, swirl, caramel, choco-everything's always gonna be fine and even better,*
> *buttery whipped, creamy, she just walked out of the realm of possibility and*
> *triumphant discourse and slow sensual saunter, you missed her by believing in your*
> *coffee order!*

DRINK IT BLACK AND GET HER!

Baby write that poem!
Rev the motor!
Live!
Don't hinder that by extravaganza-tizing this situation of only coffee!
You call...
Me?
A nihilist...
But you're the one!
Who doesn't believe!
In her! Them! Or you!
You gotta have your hidden cup o' sadness and giant, grande new supersized
loss of zone, Baby Zone.

I see a dark cocktail lounge aspect-or segment- of the show
Ladies and gentleman... An ENTERTAINER!
A troubled man
He's mad at coffee
He's sick of smug!
He don't live mild

Rick?
Yes!
I do! I'm forced to live mild!
I'm an ex-middle class guy with broke man values.
My name is 'Joshua Brokeman'.
Hi everyone!
Awesome. Awesome!

I can't do this... THIS way.
I see too much!
I've been down to the social security office.
I've been through the river of anti-realized clowns, in the idiot isle of Rite Aid.

RICK!

I'm tryin' to get laid!

By a bold woman!

Unfettered sexuality!

Untethered.

Unleashed to the actual actuality of actually, actual walking

As I'm talking

Fire and sweetness

As I write this tiny tin dicks with dickheads talk about the match maker.

"What'd ya do last night?"

Fag1000: I watched the match maker. The devil fright and anxiety dressed in…

JURY LIE

You, you were listening to something inside your head
That you had no fukkin control over! No! Control!
It was your pops fighting ya and kicking ya and then YOU remembered.
Yer fukkin Maw.
And she was always real nice
Until she switched
Like Laura here.
And she pulled yer hair.
And she lied to ya.
She fukkin lied to a "good man like you!"
You gave up yer whole life
For that fukkin baby
Cause, I mean we all know.
Women are helpless.
And they need us
And we got nothin!

Ya did it all fer, the lil nicey Jewish boys,
Only to find out that, in that one moment
Ain't no one ever! Ever! Gonna be there for yiz!
Rite?
You punk!

Yells, I'mmm theee oneee beinn honest with ya!!!!!!!!
Look at me look at me!
Don't you turn away bro, I'm here for ya, you sliced her up!
I know it! Yeah man! Yeah! Yeah! Yeah! Yeah!
Ride em bitchfucker!
Ride em you sliced that lousy cunt who wasn't never in the room in the first place
I mean all those years you pretended to like whatever the fukk she fukkin liked!
I mean what was it unfaced fears

I know, I see I see you

(TALKS TO JURY) For the first time in this man's life
You are seen
Hey, HEY, jury, fuck you !
Fuk you jury of his peers?!

(to jury) "Are you the cosmic jokers? Witnessing?
You are all fooled by your own fears.
So leave him alone.
He ain't never gonna get better
And will just kill another.
By living a lie
Let him go I say!"

You know what you need is a good…
No a cardboard box o' greatness
And just twist toss the rest of yer life
Ok! I did it!

Way. Weigh what happens when you get off. When the jury let's you off

Odd jobs and suddenly a good career, a simple girl, a small town and no more demons
man.
They tell ya shit and it's guys been believing bullshit that try so hard to believe more bullshit.
You know what you need is a good… no a heroin addiction o' greatness and an abandoned
cardboard box and just twist toss and turn around the rest of your life

She

She's beauty and she doesn't even know it
She's got bold choices, big colors.
She's bigger than life her passions, her.
I don't know.
But it's boring she's gonna be boring and small and lifeless
I mean... Where's the fighter, where's the fight?
Watch?

Excuse me, what's yer gig?
Myyyy... Don't be predictable.
We already know the choice word thing.
Weird better choices are interesting.
I don't ask anybody this question and I know ya don't believe me
There and it's irrelevant.
If you don't see; because if I'm interesting and feel, KNOW I am... than I will tell you what's
up in my world
My huge-ass realm
Not get teeny
I'm not cute
So I don't have to be, ever
You're interesting
You're... beauty

I see all that everybody's hot now.
Everybody
What ya don't like ya cover up in a tattoo or ya put an earring over here to take, to distract
Don't
Doesn't anyone get that?

They are the shit!

They are worth it
You're crazy!
No you are!
Slap me!
Inform me!
Fill me in!
I mean be interesting!

Fuck off?

Yehhh, that's the best you'll ever do
That's yer existence
Forever tellin guys to 'fuk off' and secretly wishing the guys you were with would secretly
fuck offf

See women have colors, Man.
They see the blues and they waste it on the fukkin sky appreciation, Saturday brunches
I mean nobody likes brunches nobody
But women love sexxx more than me, more than Henry Miller but they are taught to be
reasonable
I mean how wrong is it?
How?
Not wrong, but life-stifling?
Is it that women are raised by submissive women?
Who are raised by men?
Women are raised by men, men who think women should be this way or women they as a
whole should be that way

Families suck
There's a stench like hers
How you raise a kid
You say use your nose
Not sit up straight

39

Use yer eyes
Use yer nose
A parent should notice which part of the body or parts does my lil' gem bundle seem to use

Men

Men who stare at
Who aren't gay and...
Want me to stare back at them so they can take their trivial, trivial tiny egos that need love
on the indoors of a café

You walk in like this.
You, you, you walk in like this!
Look there.
Hands in the pocket.
Don't look at me
You *chill out;* Soul sucking just by looking at your anti-Nelson Mandellla.
You never heard of, much less searched and scoured the aisles of your shopping, buying
into the bullshit that doesn't even exist network.

Who are you?!
You ever ask yourself that???
Ever?
Do you?
Is there a you?
I mean it, baby fukker.
There IS you, NETWORKER.
You shopping networker, nothingness. Nothing.
And notice nothing about you that stops me
Shut life down and run from the sickened, sickness
You may come out of me!
You actually have numb nuts.

Numb nuts!

You want me to stare at you?
You.
YOu.
YOU.??!

Gonna Die

You ever see the night?
And never come back to the day?

I hear opera in this place, in his head man.
Baby tiger, cat, panther, slow saunter, ramble... ramble.
I gonna ram now
I, ahhhh, mean I don't mean nothin' baby
We gonna die
Don't it kill you man?
We, I, am gonna dieee
My lil champs we all champssss champsss
I love thattt baayyybyyy
We all champs
The rapist he gonna die
U raped by him
The thinker who never told you he loves
Heee gonna die
U gonna die
U never did the bullshit
U never gonna walk down the aisle
That fukking aisle
It's an aisle mann
Why am I gonna waste myyyy timeee
I see sooo much??
No, I seee tooo much
I knowwwww the needs inside
I couldn't find the courage?
Yes, courage
Ohhh, I love that one
Ohhh yehhhh hahaahh
Courage!

Courage!
Ohhh, this that courage over there,
There
Courage!
Right over there...

More courage

Poet Puppet

No, I don't!

Yes you do!

You want me to die.

No. No.

I don't now

Don't say that.

How can you do that?

I'm not one of your zombies out there, your rollerbladers.

I'm just jealous.

I want to have fun and I only do onstage

I'm not

Narcissistic

It's what you do. It's who you are.

How'd you know I was gonna say narcissistic?

Because I am smart and I know your proclivity for calling yourself wrong with uninformed
new age crap.

Relax brother poet. Brother puppet.

Want to look at girls?

Poet want to read paper in my poet pocket.

I. I. I. I. I mean puppet.

Puppet want to live where is flame, where is flame!

Come on ma, bro!

Let's go set fire to the men's room.

Come on baby, baby.

Where's puppet motorcycle?

Puppet want to ride.

Baby you and your puppeteer be brothers in the wind.

Puppet want to burn a hole in universe.

Puppet.

Puppet detective!

You should be more like poet.
I mean puppet.
Oh puppet poet, you poet.
You like seagulls!
Admit it!
But seagulls eat garbage.
Where you're from
Puppet want to think. Take walk alone in rain.

I like that too.

We go together.

Things

Do the wrong thing. No?

Now. Now. Now. No. No. No. No. Now. Now. Now. No. Now!

Come on man the right thing?

People always stare out the window.

I did that the **right thing.**

Always sucks. It suckkkkks.

It's a mistake and I'm tired of mistakes.

I walked by the window (my window) forlorn.

I wanna live!

Every second.

That's why I wrote.

Who would-a thought that writing was living and writing would lead me to more living and more living would lead me to more writing and life and musicians and girls, girls and guts.

Guts.

I sit around wondering what's inside of me?

Why I have to listen to the status quo?

Why?

I don't know, it's inside of me.

The ideas.

Because of money?

I refuse to believe that.

It's not even refusing.

It's stupid

They told you, **THAT** they told you.

When I was a hooker I saw the money.

Everyone's okay and they don't have to believe the budgeting couponing bullshit.

"Did your mother coupon?"

Oh, so you learned it from her and did she die rich? Did she get, get?

Did she get much less get rich?

Politician's rationale – talking to themselves.

Like people keeping themselves small.

Hey, ya gotta wait on line right?
Ya gotta do it her way and ya gotta assume what? Her way is right?
Right?
Right!
Hey, ya gotta... uhh ... when they tell ya... when you say 'excuuuuuuuuse me' it gives them the automatic response of no polite, **NO** polite, **NO** POLITE, **NO...**

I'm never gonna be the guy you want.
The guy I tried to be.
Why did I try to be that guy in the first place?
Cause I'm afraid?
Cause how could I be right?
They told me I was wrong.
They stopped me.
Don't let me any more

Light me.
Fire baby. Fire. Fire. Fire! Fire way!
Fire away!
Fire. Force. Thrust. Force. Force. Force.
Use it!
Feeling
Feeling
It's all you got
IT'S ALL OF YOU!

Oppressed

The oppression is amazing.
Ever be around someone?
When the girls are oppressed, they start to lose their own sense of anyone alive.
We become dead.
Come over well hang out.
Oh we're gonna meet to eat
Nooooo
Yes, of course
I said, see the bullshit?
SEE THE BULLSHIT
Is well… she's carrying a bag of depressed vegetables and she's going to the grocery store
and she's stoic and she thinks she's supposed to be something other than what she is, who
she is, she thinks she should be...
Dead

She thinks she's ugly and (and) she ain't…
But she's ugly in her trappings
You women are oppressed
Don't be grab n go baby, spin and grab
Don't say you used to sing, **SING!**
Be you at any fucking cost!

I knew today was gonna be bad. I knew it. I wanted it more. To happen. Something. To
happen. And the opposite of happen, happened…
Everything you don't want to happen does.

A Baptist father is hateful of others. A man you can't love fully. If you got religion you always
think there are those who don't have the right thing.
You're nervous, sweaty and you have cats that died twenty years ago and a grandmother
bedridden and she ain't aware as you that she's swimming in piss cause everybody's *just
lovely.*

I said, see the bullshit!
He holds a rock on beach!
My heart is beating too fast!
My heart is beating!

He gets up, walking in a pounding way; jumping a bit.
And he says, "I am pounding. I am throbbing.
I am throbbing, beating, my heart beats.
Larry, it beats; all my life trying to find out who I am!!
You didn't know but I been trying to find out
And I love her. I love her and that don't mean it has to do whatever people think it's
supposed to.
Oh shit, my life. I mean it looks like it's working out in a way I couldn't imagine.

LUCKY ME

Her.
She is the heat of the sun .
She's a cigarette.
It stands next to her
A lucky, and it's lit and it says smoke her.
Not me!
Go do it.
Come on man, dig her! pay attention!
If you want.

Whore

I don't like the word whore. The way these, you know little men, use it.

You're a whiney, unaware, waste of cock

If a woman's a good sexual experience don't call her a whore.

You just had an erotic sensualist give you the keys to an arena.

Take you into the realm.

Free you from the labyrinth of your acquired pseudo living habits and is now feeding your little wild crazed doggy — but you stop it and judge

All day long.

You spout dead slogans of 'I don't judge'.

Ignorance!

But a woman gives you her secrets.

Let's you lap your tongue on her skin.

Let's you taste her.

And the best you can do is call her a whore?!!

So don't judge the guy…restless entitlement, riddled networking mindset or the fitness guy calling you for extra fee… no extra fee. I work for vanity fair magazine, esquire magazine, detail-detour-dickhead-dickface-dumbface, pretty-loser-draining-face-dead-lifestyle-magazine, self magazine, hate self magazine, hate self more magazine, hang self magazine, teen magazine, teeny teen magazine, make tiny feel teenierrrr magazine.

I hung out with this girl and her eyes and her laugh when she wasn't a rigid, robot.

Instead, be afraid girl.

Be afraid girl.

Be concerned girl.

Appreciate the dull dude girl cause it's safe girl. Safe girl.

Ripped Off

He ripped me off.
They all think they can rip me the fuck off
I'm the king now
I got this huge drug deal going down and it's going down, big! With fights and guns.
And then I walk fukkkkin tall
And they can all just shut da fuk up, all of them.
Can.
Will.
Kiss it.
And do they kiss my ass?
I'm the king of the jungle world!!
I am at the top,
I'm on my way
These lil' faggots can suck my smoke, Ma'.
I'm on crush break, you think you got me???
You think that???
Fuuuucckk youuu !!!!!!!!l
Ain't never, never, going back
Every second counts
Every fuckin seconddd!!!!!!!!!!!!!!!!!!!!

Friendly

I'm friendly
I'm the friendliest
I am soo friendly!
All I ever try to be is friendly
All I want is friends. People to like me.
And when they don't, they are assholes!
I am friendly!
Me, I'm altruistic man
I'm a giver
That's what I'D do
I give

Espresso

I always like a little Sambuca and espresso

Then I needed espresso with the Sambuca and espresso

Then I needed more espresso and more espresso

And a lot of espresso

It was like I had a ah, ah, ah brain vat of espresso

A chamber

An acidic acrid abyss

A black hole bellowing for the burn

Caffeine cantata

Over the cliff operetta

Pretty soon it was any cheap espresso

At caffeine cantinas

Flights to Mexico for cheap espresso

The top heffe's of the low life labrynthian pursuit

That peak experience

That rush hour of elusive power

Ever more needing and heeding the itch

I was the bitch with the twitch for that hopped up witch

Of a Heated drink

I am Comedy Noir

Really loud
POW POW
Yeahhhahhhahhahhahh
Fuck you fuck you fuck you fuck you
Shoot shoot shoot shoot
I am comedy Noir!

I've killed people
I have begged people not to die
In the middle of the street
Even the rain hit me hard
I went to cop school
I tried cop school
I am comedy noir

I was a prostitute for your senators
I turned girlfriend's kid brothers on to heroine
Comedy Noir?

You ever fuck three 18 year olds at once, and get thrown out by the boss that was a midget because you took her mask off… and got chased around the bed, around the top of the bed, swearing to him that she didn't see me.. "Let me keep fucking her" I'm sorry sir.. racing out of the apartment, while putting your pants on
Running from a coke-head, midget, race horse owner in his penthouse apartment
You ever watch a bald very round man naked, short in a Sherlock homes hat with a pipe, lying down on a showroom floor convinced you find him alluring… con-vinced…
When you just got done telling him you chant.. Nam-myoho-renge-kyo because you are trying to change your life
So he offers $40 dollars more..
I am comedy noir

Nick Grande in a pencil thin moustache in a Ferrari — you actually took him up on his bet when said, "You think I can make 10 green lights in a row" and if I do, I don't pay for the next 10 blowjobs…

Then you find yourself holding on to his ears while he is blowing you for free and you are staring at his aquarium, angry.. with the repeated thought running through your head..

Nobody makes 10 lights in a row.. while staring into his fish tank.

I am comedy noir

I have dumped bodies, rolled in carpets

Or a body…… No… bodies

I fucked your girlfriends, when you sent them up to get the bags of heroine from me.. they bragged about their engagement to you .. they showed me pictures of you in the Jacuzzi

I carried 68 grams of heroin in the airport in Arizona.. **I put THAT on my resume**

On my way to secret meetings I would stare into Paul Newman's eyes on a video tape in a shop window, everyday and swore I would get out some day

I robbed thousands of dollars from gangsters, hit man, passed out from free-base all on one bed where the safe was.. asleep with guns under their pillows

I woke up in an unknown bed, with a check waiting for me from Halston, which read to Rudy (my hustler name)

I dropped off giant rocks of pure Peruvian for the Columbians.. with a note that says "you taste it, you're dead.." I tasted it..

I pulled cons in electronic stores and my flunky partner couldn't fit the TVs in the trunk – we were pressed for time…

I am comedy noir

Mother chicken had to talk to her hens, because one of them wasn't getting it up for the men, so I got locked in a room with a body builder, he chased me around with a lamp, til I blew him

But I pretended it was wood and I did it like the operation game

My girlfriend was a 15 year old hooker while Robert Redford's niece was interested in me, ran away again

I am comedy noir

I slide against walls at 2am

Talking to myself, saying how did I get into this again

But I would always look up and see a silhouette and I knew someday I would meet her

There was hope for a better life

But first I had to fake cry to the gangsters, til they remembered I was their son – because they could have sworn it was me that stole the money

I am comedy noir

A hit man wandering through our broken down penthouse in a mini-skirt, no one asked him why or how

I had 40 grams of heroin in front of me, fat guys with guns, left the room because they trusted me.. Enter my brother who swiped his hand through it, filled a bag and left and said fuck them

I repeated all of your secrets alone in my head, while the rain drops were now whispering to me and I could hear them

I was a scavenging coyote

But now it's **comedy noir**

Now I live out here, I actually looked at my boots and a thought flew through my head…'OH I can robe these people" .. it's just a shot in the head.. but you don't shoot them in the head.. I do.

They call it COMEDY NOIR, that's funny, I call it my life. I went down into the depths of me, came back as notoriety, I am what I pretend to be, a narcissist playing innocent, I spent every part of me, except the real me, raw sensitivity, I am the almost magician, I disappeared and almost didn't come back.

I am comedy noir

And I could use a friend.

A Ditty ... Man

Exaltation For Lack of a Better Word, Girl

Ok, I get it!
You long to live
I get it
But nobody can get ever what that really is
For you
For him
MOST people
I see now
I just want the same thing

Ohh, man I long to live
I long to live
I long to live
So what does that mean?
No.
What is that that feeling a woman shows a man: The beach, the cliff, the shooting stars?—
And she asks if he sees, if he saw one, yet — a shooting star?

"Man my cigarette means more to me" – he says.
And she likes his cigarette too, but it's different now because he thinks nothing is ultimately important
He wants to burn out and get it over with, he wants to die ...

This man me who longs to live, to touch and taste all the things that he can ever touch and taste; he is amazed but he doesn't get to keep it, EVER
He is afraid of himself suddenly
Ohh no, to be suddenly afraid of himself — the shooting stars are working on him, the cliff is calling, the lil' waves down below fucking invite him

Her eyes, her voice, her skin, her taste, her neck falling back and he is in awe of the lick

He gets to slide around and up and down each one on her tits
Her tits
Does she know being a bad girl?
Being a smart girl?
Being a fucking desiring, revved up girl?
… Is all poetry can ever triumph with

The seagulls will always fly
The life is in the girl
The girl is in the girl
The girl sits smiling, smirking
That girl SMIRK
When she sits on and in, the spit on my tongue, she laughs and she loves
EXCITEMENT AND SURPRISES

The seagull never showed his face tonight and I dropped my cigarette
She is still laughing harder. HARDER
Her eyes shoot the stars, they really do!

OH MAN THAT SMILE

The Visit

My old man came into this diner where I worked and I hadn't seen him in years, a couple, and I'm in this tiny diner and I'm wearing this coffee shop you know, attire: White shirt black tie, black vest, and I'm making milkshakes behind the counter. I liked being the soda jerk. The fountain guy. The counterman. It's like it's your domain and really it might be because you have an anxiety disorder and you think you fear people so you just stand in the cage all day and not have to deal with outside or the restaurant — Just orders and the food around you and leaning against the counter.

So, the old man comes in and he's wearing this tweed, wasp, wanna be, prestige, I'm respectable, I followed the rules that invented the idea of 'how do I get respect when secretly I hate myself! Oh!' and 'I'll raise a family on this hidden, self hatred and pleasure of phony, false, housing, lying structure, as a talking, angry, tiny, myth of tininess and call it big and ha ha! TWEED JACKET.

 Authoritative. So he stands over me and says in his fake voice, *"hiiii riiickk oh it's so good to see you."* Not realizing he never came in before. And he says *'rickkk can I talk to you? —* if he asked at all. And he says Rob, one of the idiot, repressed, denial, jew, mamas boys! said that *"you tell people I beat you."*

'Yeh'.' Me, in robot mode from his manure, mode, incurring, spell tone voice. I didn't say 'what's yer point' or 'don't come in to my work and do your shit, get out... call me or don't call me, just get out!' I yelled it under a spell — and he said *'you think I did?'*

'You did' I said. He said *'I never didn't.'*

Yeh! Ad I grabbed his lapels firmly, quietly, my hands on his tweed just holding his lil', tall, tweed jacket and I moved up to his eyes and I said 'yeah you did you beat me, you did you beat me' and he looked like a tree that nobody ever chopped once or carved anything in or pissed on — Actually like a tree that now I realize wouldn't let anyone confront again. He thought I was one of the drunk tree-pissers from his past and he walked out.

Next story.

Toys

FAO Schwartz as child
Used wooden toys and marionettes
My parents did everything
To turn me into a fagot
Not the good, gay, blow jobs in the woods, runnin' from the heteros, laffin at the rigids, the ignorant strait mutants, watchin them throw rocks at us and huggin in front of the counter guy and buying two slurpies in front of him winking, at each other kind of gay

Then him, you know, small town bigger than life, the smart fool, prince-like, king made by God rebels, knower of women and friend to what could have been a much cooler society which is in my world cause of those toys.

18-year old hooker

I was on a gay mafia cruise with a trick, as they call it and it was all these macho gay Italians in the mob and the guy who took me was this rich restaurant designer and he/we went on this cruise. I found the only girl and I made out with her all night on the main deck in front of everyone... all night long.

Before that there was a BBQ on a cliff and I was on the beach below and I was running and running, just hating my life and this seagull flew over head and he was faster (obviously) and he turned around and hovered over my head — as if he knew I needed to see and talk to him. So I asked him, I said to him, "When? Know someday, I'm gonna be free — and I am."

So the next day the trick and his wife calls me into their apartment and says his wife and him, THEY, want to talk to me and he plays this Doctor Doolittle song—the one about the seal, Dorothy. The name of the song was 'twenty thousand years of pain' and he plays it and he cried and said his wife and he said the song is about me and I'm in my denim lil' denim jacket with the American flag.

Someday, I'm gonna be free.

Bold Man

Bold man walks saunters swaggers around apartment

ASHTRAY: "Bulls-eye, man u never miss!!!!!!"

      "Look at you shine-in!"

      "Smokin!"

      "Burnin!"

      "Sweet unashamed unabashed, bold gold!"

      "Mannn you tear it up with your infinite being right here!"

      "Right now!"

      "Baby smoke that cigarette, you'll never get cancer

      "Only and constantly, always, every time... BULLSEYE!"

"Keep going! Don't never stop. The world must have you"
"Hey, Cig, tell 'em and look'em in the eyes man"

CIGARETTE: "We don't have to tell you ever. You know always and in all, every single
way. Go baby go, awww, your given, you give and your always interesting,
amazing, awesome, true and awesome and you always get what you fucking want
and it comes to you and you grab it! And go and go! MORE!

Always, more with you. Life and excitement. How do you do it swing that shirt?

SHIRT: "Ohh man, when it comes to choice, YOU ARE THE CHOICE MAN, powerful! Ah
ahhhh, self assured is neurotically insecure compared to you." "And they always
compare themselves to you and I get to ride on yer back. Man you put me on! Man,
he's wearin' me, that's right! He's goin' out with me on him!"

Jacket: "Oohh, I feel so cool and successful on you. Everyone else needs the shirt or jacket
for this feelin' but I, the jacket of choice, your bold choice, feel exciting on you.

Your Boldnesss.

PICK ME! PICK ME!!

Corruption Fun

You wanna make friends with everybody

HER: You gotta try these meatballs, mmm, k?

HIM: What meatballs? Waddya mean, wha?

HER: You never had meatballs? Well this is gonna be your first time. This way.

HIM: Eat'em off her. Lift da cloth. Lift it you fat, dumb, greasy, wop, fuk!

(looks at Rick – laffs).

HER: Ha Ha Ha Ha!

HER: I can say anything I want and they get it. ***This ain't the states right, comic***?

HIS HEAD: I mean it is but you're here now with us and we get you. Question is, do you get us? If you don't that's a whole different, uhh, scenario! Now eat 'em off. Eat da meatballs off the beauteous, as you like to say curve of her back… you dumb acting, phony, intense, driven ambitious, freaked out, elitist - without wanting to be smarter than everybody else, fucking nervous lil' scrawny pussy

HIM: Everyone's scrawny, more driven and smarter and you ass fuck layer so garage door SUV very big suburban butt.

Her: Eat'em you wanna get darker, more corrupt, look-it, I'm your new manager.

Rick: Look at it, treat it dat way. Okay? You adorable lil' cartoon skunk

Swivel Slowly

I frump around and seep out shitty self hate
I just look at the computer screen
I swivel slowly, inadvertently in my structures is life.
Life and realize there is nothing in my within my structures - just make like I got something going…

Ya know! The rent! The rent! The rent!
Knowing I am doing the rent walk!
The seething, slow, sluggish, boiling of broiled egg fists in a row from previous fights with other men who hated me, fiercely, wickedly, wasting their lives.
Their lives?
They have none and neither me, but for some reason I think/feel and study.
They stare in amazement.
Life to them might as well be, well it might as well be the basement
BUT NOT FOR ME!
I am going to live in a car! To celebrate my thoughts!
My feelings, long dead are living again!
And will writhe in their shit for now, but now always changes for me why not for them?
They are smug to others!
They will kill me!

Say baby!

Man I feel awkward and creepy!
I feel the need for an aloof Swede!
I'm tired of you Americans
I hear the fear! Baby!
Say baby, Baby
Remember when you used to lower your jeans and say I don't give a fuck, baby!
Say baby! Baby!
Give it to me straight! Outta the gate! Play fool sex, baby?
I've played fool for the illusion of rules
It don't work for them 'n it ain't working for you
Right outta the gate, BABY
This ain't no job interview!
Don't wait for me or the Lord to tell you what to do!
I ain't growing up and he ain't showing up!
Don't worry you'll confess
But won't admit it was the best
You'll always keep secrets in your Easter dress
It's the way you say baby that lets me hear for one night no fear
See the way you say baby drives me thru the woods of this wasteland and makes me…
I hear the calling of all men falling
But the one who stands and walks it, like he talks it
I can't stand bein' without the man whisperer
I'm goin into madness now
A beautiful high dive, in to the dive itself
My balls no longer on the shelf!
I ain't no made smaller by this countries messages

Truths

Henry miller!
When I read Henry miller it stopped time
The waste of time
Tryin to be good all the time
Tryin to do right so I could be right!

Hey, its panic time
Good morning and guess what yeahhh!
Waste o' time
How ya doin?
No jokes cummin' up?
Nooo, noo, noo, just memories
O' how wrong you are.'
CHOICE??!!
You don't know what choice is!!!
IT'S OVER!
And here's the 'it's over demon'
Yeahhh, I look like an angel, don't I?
Ohhh, here comes my 'I dance like an angel, Demon'!

No one's gonna save you
You can't be saved
Redemption is a myth and you been believing' it too long
Here are the real furies!!
Loser.
You idiot.
You think God's gonna help you
Yer dead in twenty years
Sooo what?
Come on man dance around like you got cancerous moths and little greasy, sick, fish,
jumpin' and flittin' around like a thousand babies with pissy dicks
Feel yer sinner self
You know yer insides

Man with pissy shit!

Oh, here's redemption

Ohh nooo. Less gigs

Think small here's the 'think small demon'

Hey, hey, go after the girl

You don't want

And dream about the pain of being with her!

Ohhh scroll down yer phone all day, hour after hour

Rehearse the speech of being firm and how... ohh here comes 'The worry demon'

Ohhh, how can I make them see I need the money and it gets me to entertain and even reveal hidden... Uhh... stuff

TRUTHS

Air Guitar Playing Manager

It's cause of your cute blow jobs
You got to fight for your right to never wear Ed Hardy
Welcome to the awkward and creepy party
I took a shit on the cast of twilight!
They didn't move inhuman zombie LA actor groove!

Stone washed jeans
Dog shit on the front!
Piece of a pen stickin' outta ya head

I can't use the register, my boss won't let me open the register!
Sayin' things twice. Listen! LISTEN!
Add a stammer.
Confuse low self esteem for nice!
It's okay, you can hire me I'll never ask for a raise!
That someday I'll be a rewarded haze!
Don't need no raise! Just glad you don't fire me!
Hey, you're a loser boss!
Make fun o' me, in your Hawaiian shirt!
Playin' air guitar by the coffee machine
I'll be late, but I'll stay late

Good, Bad, Ugly, Gorgeous

Demons at door and wise, wisdom ass pearls!

Hey man how ya doin'?

Yeah, come on

Hey man don't trust yourself

Hey man, yeah yeah. You know it's horrible

What everybody says about everybody

What is everybody gonna do?

Hey, man put me in your arm

Come on.... What does anybody matter? Ever. Ever. Ever.

Come on they are takin' over

Hey your good, bad, ugly, and gorgeous

You're hot man. You got it movin' and you just got to release it baby

Put your hand on her leg!

Man, touch her face! Man!

Tell her you wanna see her naked

Do it YOUR way

THEIR way sucks

Everybody else's way sucks the rat shit outta horseshit and their lives are shit, not just shit but stupid cowards

Be judged man, be judged by everybody

Worry Altruism Holding Back

I'm tired of always holdin' back in this country and when I let go the lil' jealousies talk tiny turd shit

Why is it, it's like maybe I'm a rapist

If I like you so much, maybe I'm a food addict

Maybe I'm a life addict

Maybe I'm impatient

Maybe, I'm not altruistic enough or maybe I'm not altruistic at all

Maybe I'm a genius

Hey maybe I'm brilliant

Hey you're like a lil' boy

Hey you're spoiled

Hey you're amazing

Hey I'm nervous around you

Hey hey hey all the heys and maybes

Do I wanna skateboard?

Do I wanna write?

Why does life always feel like shit!

Who cares?

Who cares?

Who cares?

Who cares?

Ooh you care Rick and who cares Rick and why is it all ultimately so boring....

Soo soo soo boring!

Demon

You set it up so you wouldn't have to care
Hence, neither would they
Nor did they
Nor could they care
You Rick, YOU
Shut up! You ain't no demon! Demons hang out!!!!!!
They lift your head up OFF THE TABLE!!
And bring really cool ass, hot ass, steamin' ass, swaggerin' hookers to ya! Or exes! Or the
final wife trying to revive ya as A *12-YR OLD GIR*
Or.... If u were a real real really demon...as a lil' 8 yr old girl who you'd get turned off by at
ZERO HOUR!
Just as you peruse their bodies!
BUT! The twelve year old takes ya by the hand into the bedroom, AND yer ex-wife says "*I
know baby, I knowww*"
And, her brother pisses on ya cause he now can't stand you at all
And the ex says anybody can see he's wrecked up!
AAAAALLL... Torn up inside!
No! That much understanding would be God!
The demon has her YOUR EX touch yer hair that has sweat and tears on it
And she lifts her skirt n tries to get fucked by you
"Come stick it in me before he comes back up with the meds"
And u accidentally curse her out
That turns her on until you say something (you always wanted to slaughter the bad ex with),
and ya tell this one BY SOME QUIRK O'ACCIDENTAL DESTINY FILLED FATE! (you know
the thing you wanted to... you know tell the other one !)
SO now! This one's gone! And! They leave ya alone to die!
Motherfukker die baby die die die baby die

I Do It All For You

You mother fucker you were my best friend!

That's like bein made in the fuckin' mob

The goddamn mob!

You were my best friend

I had plans I was hopin' to tell you everything. EVRYTHING!

Then you bring your stupid moralistic wife into the fukkin picture and your wearin' Ed Hardy hats, shirts and cologne!

You fagot

You are the worst kind of fagot (he holds guy up beaten and delirious!)

You fuck (he stabs him again, you ain't the good kinda fagot)

Yer the worst kind

You go to church and yer married and you don't suck dick, unless you buy it!

No heart!

You are afraid of yer fukkin heart!

If I was gay

I'd be lovin' it all over the fukin world!

Instead of waiting for one lame! Lame! Actually really lame! Mentally thwarted cunt to call, discuss and go out with me!

Cop dances with wife and they kiss

She says I'm so proud of you

You're a good, good man

Cop: *I do it all for you, all fer you*

He thinks back to hooker OD-ing

I killed three guys tonight, I do it all fer you

Then cop-to- cop, ***I do it all fer you***

He sees kid bein' mocked

He runs over beats da crap outta guy n picks up his son

I love you son, I do it all fer you

Seeking Approvals: Found in Hotmail and Sent to Adrian

Poem

Ohhh the beauty
Ohhhhhh (on his knees) the beauty!
I never knew I had a poet's heart
Dies when beauty slaps him
Lays pulsating ever so silently
My adorable heart
My sweet heart waiting in the wings
Hidden all its life
My silent dying, nurturer
Whispering
Always taking me to providence
I made it wait
I learned to apologize for its fear
It hid in panic from it the falseness
I learned the training-days and nights the bunker of shit
It only could go where I would
Or so it seemed

Twenty

She's twenty
I'm older, a lot!
        I like you
You do?
        I like your dick
You do?
        Mmm hmm, I like your voice
Why?
        Because it sounds like you smoke
Yeah, I like your voice
        I like your mustache
You did? But I don't have one anymore...
        I don't care, I like you
What happens when I'm seventy five?
        I'll suck your dick
Yeah? Yeahhh....
        Yeahhh, I like you
I love you

Angry stripper

You ever see an angry stripper dance?

The furrowed brow so furrowed — her angry, ensuing, danger, depression, tank eyes, brows. And she leans forward with a scowl; frozen in position for centuries and moves her head and nothing else like this and her clitoris looks like the forearm of an angry polish dockworker.....

The stripper who kept telling me "Lenny would never treat his girlfriend like this!"

And I would keep pushing her to talk about Chomsky, because I saw the book in her car and all she talked about was her résumé for being a stylist.

And I said "how come we never talk about Chomsky or politics?"

And she would yell out loud unrestrained "I feel judged! I feel judged!
Lenny would never treat his stripper girlfriend like this!"

And finally said, "WHO'S Lenny?"

And she said "Lenny Bruce." And she said "Lenny Bruce would never treat his girlfriend like this!"

And I said "Lenny was stoned on heroine 24 hrs a day, all day and night! I'M NOT. I gotta hear everything you say!!!

"I
HEAR
YOU!"

Choose

Would you order a sandwich from me?
I'm the guy who you know not to
I'm the guy who is standing, asking you, what you want, but giving you the finger behind the counter

Well, actually that isn't true

I'm the guy who I was hungry and homeless and in psych wards and a thief and a prostitute so I am the true to himself, at any fucking cost artist...

So I know what it means to be hungry

So actually I always put more than the fucking gauged, metered out, corporate rip-off portions

Unlike the lil' roly-poly, true believer, ass-kiss manager would spew on me and jump in say "1/1: A scoop of tuna, half a scoop ! Ok? Ok?"

So, one time I put extra cheese on this sandwich and the customer leans forward smiles big and says "Yo, you gangsta with that cheese bro.

You Gangsta!

I said "there's nothing GANGSTA about this, it's just cheese on a sandwich, there's nothing exciting about this moment between you and me it's never gonna be anything but a slice of cheese. That's all it's ever gonna be. You eatin' cheese. That's probably all its ever gone be for you. Little slices of cheese in your life!"

They called it an 'upscale sandwich café.'

There was nothing upscale. It's a deli. That's what it is and that's what it was. A deli!

The pig wasn't invited. They didn't see him dance or pig-out at Juilliard and say "we saw you in the ham sandwich recital and we love your work! Would you please be on our sandwich? We adore you. Can we slaughter you? It would be an honor!"

It's ham. That's what it was, ham…

And people would come in all pretentious, but they'd always have that lil' gesture that gave away who/what they were and how their lives were gonna turn out…

These guys, would come into this upscale deli on their cell phones. This upscale deli, where workers did long lengths of time at Rikers Island and were placed here to work—in my case I was from a psych ward. The guys, the little big business men, were on their iPhones, impressing the annoying, hounds-tooth blondes next to them on line, at this upscale deli.

" Tell Speilberg too, its twenty million or nothing. Tell Microsoft its fifty billion dollars or nothing. Tell DiCaprio he can suck my dick! I'm going to my summer house after my upscale meal… It's made out of a thousand golden… NO MY HOUSE! My house, it's made of a thousand golden kayaks, a thousand golden kayaks…" And then the gesture…

No, no, no, no. Honey mustard. I said honey mustard.

And there/then the finger point. As if trying to ring the teeniest bell so as not to wake the sleeping gentle rodent in the bell.

No, no, no, no. Honey mustard. Eeww spinach artichoke? A side of that? Can you wrap it and unwrap it and slice it again and recycle it and add teeny mushrooms again and again and again for the rest of my routine-out, dullness, of a no-mirror, to ever see myself, nonexistent life!

I used to work in a sandwich shop.

People Who Wait

You ever see people who wait on line at a restaurant?

I mean a meal dump-like theme restaurant

I mean a Denny's?

A low-end theme restaurant

Like THEY'RE WAITING on line to meet a President or see a float of their once small idiocy

floating by

They don't even know they've assumed this position

They just stand there

You are waiting

It's like sheep or cows in a field

It's like those cruelty to animal things, where they don't know the banks are milking 'em

while they wait on line

Cliff hanging

I'm a pretty intense guy
I mean, I'm used to hanging
I mean what I say
I mean, hangin' cause I said it
Hangin' over a clifff with nothing but my demons holdin' me in mid-air
Laughing and screaming, trying to scare me
More than fallin' off a clifff
Nothin but those ugly, never tiring, monsters of gargantuan-misnomered-anomalies of outsider-beguiled-ness
These hideous true beauties to which the only loyalty I have
Lemme make it simple for yiz
I'm used to choosin,' hangin of the cliff of life
Nothing but my demons holdin' me in mid-void
Sayin, "sure we gotcha pal," Screamin' this!
I choose the rapture of the bad, badass, ass ballet
When I fuck it's because I love that sinking feeling
Or diving lusciously into a book, my writing, painting, conversation or the back of the vagina
I'm not a gamer
A shopper
A TV watcher
I choose possible ruin at every turn and leap!

I like studyin' GIRLS

I like studyin' girls
The way they do little things
The way rub their ankles together when waiting for coffee
This tough little business girl on the phone, still rubs and actually plays with her ear and tugs lightly at her hair
Playfully she's rubbing her ear as her long, slender free, girl fingers stick out of the strands of her long stringy gorgeous hair

Men just sit
No characteristics
Even this gay guy next to me

I mean we gotta be stoic
We gotta be tough
What happens if you're not?
What if I'm in a fight and I sat next to these guys who wanna FIGHT ME?
I say, with the pride of ancient Indians mocking Vikings, "I'm NOT TOUGH! I'M NOT TOUGH"
No? But I'm gonna hit you
No, I'm not tuff. It's unnecessary. It's not needed in this situation.

Now, with explosive pride, but leaning into his face, I say: "I'm scared. I'm very frightened of you and I'm ok with that. YOU WIN."
Your, uhh… you're you. Oh, what's it called… ummmm…. Tuff
I'm not
You're stronger
You can lift bigger things
Yes, you can knock me down
You!
I'm tellin' you.. YOU are able too
You'd be able to hurt me

Yes, so now, what's gonna happen if I don't, stare at you, or if I do?

Just smile.
Touch my chest, breathe and say *"hey, it's so cool to try and get you to...* SAY HI TO ME"
To get you in bed or maybe even fall in love

You wanna try?

Tool

Success?
Broadway show?
Oh, I don't wanna bug him
There's no such thing as success
But there is running away
My tool is in the evidence
Symptom, A RESULT

Pussy and Thought

She speaks in lavender book cover slogans
It's all about a plant
I gave you fruit, you give me something!
This ain't the twilight of my life, Buddy
This ain't *Twilight*
I don't need or want kids (gummy worms with dead eyes), or sweaters or cold medicine
I need pussy and thought
PUSSY AND THOUGHT
But all the tepids tell you how to do shit and ya get confused
You let yourself get confused
So, the battle starts now
Their battle is always on
And their war is harder than yours
Their war is always insidiously stupid

Influences

They put Vaclav Havel in prison
Writer
Artist
Jail fucker
Then he's in charge of the Czech Republic
A prime minister
Nobel peace prize winner
I thank Nelson Mandela
People are afraid of how big they are, not how small they are!
Nikos Kazantzakis wrote Zorba the Greek
Last Temptation of Christ
He lived with Ghandi and Castro
They studied me for years
Walked side by side
"I stared at the mountains with my insatiable eyes"
That expression never leaves me, it pulls me out of the grave
These are men I learned from while letting guys blow me for heroine and tacos or sixty
dollars wherever your self esteem was and mine neither and both
Not to mention Paul Newman in the HUSTLER
CARLITO'S WAY

You ever have a CARLITO'S WAY moment with a vagina?
When you're hustling and your straight you tend to appreciate/revel in your own sexuality
that you finally get to have
I sucked so much dick there wasn't enough pussy in the world to make up for the stifled
artist I am
Not enough beauty in the world
We are all going to die trying
So fucking go, Baby
Go.

The Fuck You Magician

Every day it's down to the wire
Every second I bring the fire
Lighting up your home with all my desire
My eyes awake as I watch you
Watch me eat your cake
Thanks for the meal now what's the deal!
I spent my life trying to heal
The only lie left to believe
Every self help trick up the Gurus sleeve
I'm the fuck you magician
I just say fuck you and you used to disappear
Now you know I'm really begging you to stay here

Is

I'm that IS which is destroyed in life
This country
I need
He needs
He lives for the moment and the moment kills him and doesn't yet know that what kills him,
makes him more unbelievably strong
He is not what the word,
Your world is told to believe
He is exempt of being exempt
He has nothing to give
As you call, give
His unleashed differentness
His unleashed-ness is unleashing you

lil prOstitute

When your straight and your with men for years
There's not enough pussy in the world to cover up that wound
When I see a woman
I see the girl
I see the woman
I see the femininity
Their eyes
The curve of their face
The way they have these little fucking nuances
When their mouth moves to create a smile
When they stand and pull up their zipper
The way they play with their zipper on their coat
Here. Look. Look
And their hair…
The ones whose hair is unwashed
They put the several strands in their mouths and chew it when no one is looking
And the way they shift ON THEIR FEET
And their choice in clothes/colors

Oh, the secrets I've seen
When they take their clothes off
I shed a tear

Sick Stupid Demented Childhood

When I was a little boy
I don't remember too much except being alone
Watching Match Game with one of my brothers
Knowing I was not living my life
Knowing
Waiting
Thinking …
Somehow, I will get out of this shit-headed family of funk monkeys

I mean I was an alive boy
I was born
I was born but the beatings man, the whippings with the belt, the independence taken
away…
No control
There was only drinking and pot
I remember going to see the Godfather alone, but with the maid the great Vivian (she was
also squashed)
Too much man
Too much crap
Over-protected
But something else

I remember brother twin having a girlfriend
And thinking how did that happen
I wasn't allowed to go out with girls and how did he even know too?
I was with him every day I never saw them together
I was around him every day
NOW
I think there were secret covert meetings
No one talked to me!
I sweated when I asked someone out
Goddammit!

Im sick of being a non live-r

A Reason to Stay

Baby gimme a reason to stay!
Get rid of the reason!

With your power
Baby swing slow and think
Think
THINK
Ohhh, she sighs
So think about a sigh wrapped, intertwined with all the femininity in the world
Stifles!
She likes to get choked?
No! She wants something a man can only put into words
After her force is released
Living her femininity too, her force

To true catalysts:
Opposing lovers entering the cardboard world
O' unhappy responsibilities
As a man looks out his window wishing he stayed with her but in the end his career almost
took off
It really mattered to him
Until he met her and now walks the street for one kiss
One fuck
One experience
That is an experience, an experience instead of metered out caution!
You ever fuck caution?
That's all it is and I never got past that!

Humanity

Awkward and creepy?
That or a racist looking for agreement for his sorry ass, stupidity and dick-headed desire?
To spread hate!

Racist to do list:
Go to Kinkos, K-Mart: Buy containers. Staples: Buy bins
Squint my eyes when a "race" walks by especially if HE'S doing financially better than me
Talk down to an immigrant
Hate Jews
Secretly cry when I realize I hate women because I admire them so much
Lookie lookie
If you have this look in your eye when a race walks by, you are a racist!
FIGURE IT THE FUCK OUT

Finally, this is your shot to say *"it ain't the fundamentalists"*
It ain't the militants
The home schoolers
It's me!
I'm the racist, right?
RIGHT!

Right here. Right now
NOW!
Right now you useless pig, figure it out
Don't be like—*hand to chest,* "You know sometimes I have this *Hatred* for a race?"
Oh my, I really surprise myself!

Do something right now
Lookie lookie
A Negro
A Chinamen
A Jew
Or a politician

I'm so sick o these idiots, jerking off these faces
These explosive world destroyers with just a HELLO
 I'm so angry about my FUCKING CAREER

My-self-fuckng-doubt
Every time I'm about to do something
Myself doubt fucking brings its own dresser and sits on top of it and says:
"I'm here. I'm here. Hey. Hey. Look at me. Look at me. LOOK AT MEEEEE, LOOK"
That could help someone?? Someone??

Read a book, hula hoop!
Lick an ice-cream cone
Have anxiety sex
DON'T DO ANY OF THAT
Just be the walk-around-clown in dickhead town

DO

You can see the rules as they walk by you
The stiffs standing against the wall wondering how it all happened
Not knowing its cause
They believed and wanted
You believe the moth-ridden slogans
Farting strongly out of weak dead, sheep's mouths

Meeting People

Long tall cool one
This your lady, Man?
If you was my angel baby I'd tear you up
You be smiling like
Aaahhh aaahh
Come on man!
I know you two got a good thing!
No one ever said I didn't say you wasn't a beauteous couple with all the happiness you both deserve
I'm just trying to meet people

You know baby
You know
Yeaahh, Still ain't met the man you so long for?
I know, Man
You're the deal-e-oh... oh oh!
I am sayin' something wrong?
Yeah, what's right?
YOU TELL ME
CHOSEN MA, ALL WALKS
You tell me (mean) mother fucker!
You tell me
Being alone all night long!
Damn it!

Yeah, if there is a God he wants me to be the cool, angry, loner!
Baby, you're the ass slithering represent – NO!
The EMBODIMENT! Of all man kind's belief
Man, you are the exciting unrequited symbol of desert!
You. The real lick-able cupcake!!
Mannnn, if you ain't the unheard thunder! The unheard thunder!
The unheard thunder resounds inside of YOU!
Never screaming your own sex truth of erotic desires!

I'm finishing your unheard thoughts
You got dissatisfaction in the form of an agitated, lonely panther
Ahhh ah ah!

LEMME FINISH, Man!
We are trying to have a conversation – an exchange of ideas!
Man 17 poems already written
Two hundred paintings and a bottle o' wild pills
All in your lonely physicality
Descend passion hawk, DECEND

The Moon and Me

Nobody's up except the moon and me
So I was a hooker
I say that for no reason except it's the only time I remember
I don't remember my childhood
I don't remember the 18 years in AA
I don't remember my so called family and friends
Nobody
NOBODY
All I ever did was watch people get over me
THE MOON

Faithful

I'm trying to be faithful to the morality of others and be a nice guy!
I'm trying to focus on my career
But when a poet sees you walk it's insane
The madness grins and looms
Bang. Bang!
I see your feet like a hidden musician hears, the beat
A smarter than hell junkie starts itching!
The good boy starts bitching!
The drums
The drums
Boom boom, Baby
Boom boom!
My hearts beat is waking me, stirs me alert!
Comedy is boring
Your story languorously alluring
It lures me
Boom boom boom boom!
Make room the silky
Confusion croons and the silky confusion looms
Boom! Wow! Baby wow!

What the almost fuck in hell!

Hell is almost fucking!

An Old Prayer

Dear god.
I pray for the knowledge of your will
For me
The power to carry it out (I'm on my knees before I grab the mic"
Breezed fur of some image of the coyote
A coyote dancing on a hill, scavenging, starts to appear
I focus
Dark road and some black fur with breeze blowing through it appears now
As I write this

HEY PRAYS: *"God grant me the serenity to accept the things I cannot change, the courage to change the things I can and he wisdom to know the difference"*

Relax!
Get hyped up!
Feel your intensity, passion
(PS on my knees) Doing these prayers ..
Later on I would do 'em standing up – before approaching the stage
Your head sometimes becomes the coyotes head with glare and wild knowing and not knowing or caring to know
Who cares, it's my world?
Smile and who cares about the world?
It's duplicitous

He repeats the 6th step prayer from AA:
"My creator
I am now willing that you should have all of me
Good and bad
Take away my difficulties
That victory over them may bear witness to thy power, thy love, and thy way of life
May I do thy will
Always
Amen"

The coyote is now on the top of the hill, mountain
Feet, hooves, paws, dancing, this way and that
In the sand and dirt
Kickin' it up and in his own way

Dancing coyote
Dancin'
Scavenging!
Comes up stage before dancing
First he's going to garbage containers
The old wire ones on the street corners
HE'S A COYOTE
You're a coyote as you breathe deeper and deeper not to be fooled by this fake world
False concerns on stage, perhaps in life
Yes in life and then he's laughing , that beautiful hard hyena laugh
Rolling around in the dirt
He is the hyena and becomes the coyote again
Roll your head, hard and release!

He's on stage!!
He sees God, *HE IS THE COYOTE*

Her Face

On an airplane
I keep drawing this girl's face
Her eyes
Her lips are an intricate mountain of beauty
I've never seen eyes, lips and then
The glimpse I caught of her neck, her eye lashes
When her eyelashes come down it's like the rain sliding and jumping off the cliff of a BLINK!
Her eyes crystals, blue longings
She's fuckin' hot!
And she lingers when she looks and you are struck
Fucking struck by her lightning quick flashes
She is lightening quick flashes
LIGHTENING QUICK FLASHES
Her eyes pour liquid fire
Pushing you against a wall
The force of her eyes
THE FORCE OF HER EYES
She draws **IN DETAIL** like some guys snort **SPEED!**
She's an artist - and does she know?
She sees!
Not just studies that would be a waste of her ... life
She is a free girl, a woman!
For her, if you are reading this…
Cough

Old Journal

"I got something banging in me man
He's in Wells Fargo robbing a bank
 I need my needs met now baby
John Voigt in the Champ
　　　What about my needs
　　　What about what I want?
Faye Dunaway... uhm!
John Voigt: *Grunt, downward arms thrust towards the ground*

A man walks into the room, holiday dinner with a bunch of fat turkeys (not judging, that's
how they are)!
Or the same man in a room of coked-up and horny girl business associates
Another man with heroined-out hookers, squatters
Another man making love to a homeless woman
Another man, Me with Angela Stone in the Best Western
Another man in a room with his magic girl reading his shit
She cracking him up and he is being surprised
Another man alone in a room with a psychotic clone face, spray painted on his weird, extra
bright, yellow painted wall
He is writing this stuff, rubbing his head and he says don't wonder why I'm writing this - just
write it!
Another man in the room, the other room, hoping to get his Father's approval
　　　No!
　　　Getting it at hyper-speed
　　　Can your father?
　　　That father.
　　　A father ever really be proud of his son?
　　　Yes…

Some male floating by
A fairy stays on his cloud
There were fathers out there

No!
Do things, so an old man, one day dead, after he's gone, who's proud now?
Or are you unendingly excited for what you do today?

Another room
Another man

The old man dying or conscious that he's gonna be dead and he considers his past choices
and writhes in anger over how his son accomplished those things that would make him
proud but he isn't.
He's just angry that his son did more, moved beyond the old man, but the old man realizes
his son didn't.
He was just bragging about his "fitting in" and "showing off" but neither of them found
passion and guts.
Goddamn-it, God what am I?

Am I not a leader? A free thinker?
Why did I hold back and teach my son to hold back!
Or this is as good as it gets?
You know *"you do the best you can and can't complain"*
Whose gonna listen?
More turkey and another man?
ME!

Amnesia

To all those who are mad at me
I had amnesia
I actually, really did
This is my truth
I don't remember you
If I do all details are latent in my mind

I'm the only one on your side
I know you didn't do it
But nobody else does
Nobody else knows how to truly give a person a second chance
They think it's a fucking handshake!
They think "ok, I'll say hi to you"
But no one will fight for you
Hell, you won't even fight for you
And when you do, you got apathy personified
Man from the mist
Really, the miasma!
Rising apathy from the depths of death
Hell!
You get it because everybody out there wants you to slowly be dead in slow motion with
them!
They don't know "what's the use?"
Yet you go with them
And you try to have faith in them
The lawyer
Activists
But they don't know corruption

There's another way out and it's me

Award

Rick Shapiro accepts his Academy Award for skinniest, hedonist, most expressive, ex-middle class, searching loser, expansive, exclusive, complex and most intricate, street punk, dreamer of lustful/loving knife fights in parking lots, romancer, leg licking, non-threatening threatener, who says the audience doesn't feel threatened thing and poetic, lyrical, erotic, amphitheatre of eroticism, screamer from deep within the darkest crevice of the mermaid cafe type-award with unseen, un-noticed fought for characters woven in and unleashed award. Uhh and also the Academy's Award for smartest, self-educated, **blurter of carrier of shamanistic**, no "I'm just a guy," heated discourse, freeing new ideas and wolf eaten by coyotes while eating the wolves spirited making award.

2005

Don't Stop

All my life
Told
Where to stand
Stiff and scared
In grey flannel pants
Thinking
Told to stop thinking
Shut up
Mocked by my own father
Now I still let people hold me the fuck back
Krakouer comes to mind (Ass-kiss, insect)

Where am I?
Why do I need so much protection?
Like I believe them instead of myself
I have survived everything
I'll certainly survive the next thing — THIS!
But I won't speak up!
Always tired
Always trying to burn myself out
Mama taught me to feel too burnt out to worry!!
I was the most scared child you ever saw or that was how I felt inside or was taught to act
Taught to act
TAUGHT TO ACT!!
I was taught to act
But inside I was wild, brave, caring, sensitive and free and none of that was going to hurt
me

See, I didn't know in life there is pain

You got hurt but you also triumph constantly

Now I watch the other guys just show up and just move on!

Ahead

Move ahead or even and even just let themselves relax and live life their own life!

I mean I do it too

It's just that I have to keep asking and I always or constantly stop myself

Atheists and trannies

I admire two types of people

Atheists and trannies
Trannies say they are gorgeous women while the wimpy-as so-called men and women run
around sayin 'that's a man!
That's a mmmaaannnnn!!
Damn it!!
Damn him, her, she, it!!
Asshole!
Asshole!!

Atheists go around saying, quite clearly:
There is no god I think for myself
While tight ass Americans run around, saying:
There is a God
Oh, he doesn't believe in God—or— I'm in the program and God is good, I've seen him
Or I'm a good Christian, mislead, corrupt jerk!
He don't believe in no God
No good

I mean, where would we be?
Without god!

Work Ethic

I notice some girls have this work ethic or how to be a good woman look n their eyes
Although to me the word ethic looks like their father in their eyes
That 'forceful, I admire him solely, because my mother was such a care taking, wimp and he
is the only other example that was thrust into me in my surrounding' eyes
The arena where they are taught to be a good daughter is taught to be good
She enters the ring and is kissed by her father
These people
With the work ethic look in their eyes are in the way of the people with love and ambition
Love and ambition? I mean vision in their eyes
I mean the ones who play with and at life at all times
It seems all times
I was never allowed to play as a kid
Only to impress or to show how I follow rules to show other, retarded, stilted, thwarted,
murdered, cowards how they were able to beat me up and down
As long as the dermatologist beat me down
As long as I was scared by the angry stupid, neighbor
As long as I knew that we were better, richer, more well-mannered Jews
As long as we were also quiet and waspy and charming Jews
As long as — was the rule
As was the religion
As fucking long as... with no contingency

You were dangerous, you would lose
If no fear of retribution
If no fear of bigger forces was in your fucking, hearing eyes and skull like fore frontlets
between thine fucking eyes
I kiss it before I enter the fucking house and before I leave it
What the hell does that do to someone's system
All that fear
All those lies
All that superstition super-fuckin-stition.

I have to bend down and kiss it

I have to lean forward and dobbin and pray and hate the ones who don't have my religion

They might hate me

They might hate me for they don't understand how fucking important my devotion to nothing is

They see that you are a coward

Perpetuating cowardice and keeping yourself stupid!

That's what all dogma does!!

Comic: I'm sick of this religious government

All perpetuated other peoples, bored, forced, ignorant beliefs, un-evolved, uninvestigated, unfeeling

Just stupid cowardice

And they create whole nation states around it!

It's George W

As a little boy listening to his hick, silver spoon, parents, who sit like losers, listening to priests

Little faulty men

Simple

Schmuckcs

Like you and me

A wrathful God?

Cut the shit!

Jesus wants us to perpetuate democracy

No, he wants you to open Halliburton boutiques

He wants us to run third world countries to the ground

Our charitable hearts want to give you 50 cent an hour wages

Gimme a break

But first we have to bulldoze Palestinian houses

It's the promised land

God promised us

He's making promises for us

So bomb the civilians

To Audience Member

I see you with your angelic yet dirty hair
The hunger in your eyes
But I got other things on my mind
Like, why democrats and republicans are scumbags?
Afraid to do anything with their lives except keep their travel perks
Why money corrupts?
Why everyone in LA has to look so perfect?
Is it that everyone is afraid to be alone?
Which if comfortable and finally accepted *"we are ultimately alone "*
Would this lead us each to be a *'CATALYST FOR CHANGE'*?
Would this lead us?
We would choose to stand alone in power and passion
Or does a good hooker kill that itch?
I mean a continuum of hookers and we're never alone
Until that coyote-esque, stealthy, nasty, wonderful, little, blast of rapturous confusion with torturous truth sneaks up from within us again?

I see you
That fantasy
You bent over the back of yourself
Adored thighs tan and homogenous-ness
Bring me to the conventional knees
Kneeling under you
Longing to just fit in into your life

I'll lie to you
But I gotta think about that little boy in me
Who is he?
Socialism?
And my girl who keeps throwing that phrase out there
Socialism

Get Out

There's no getting out
There's no escape
You can't get me out
I'm in here
I've gotten in always
In where people's ideas are in or out
People are always in

Your life is now *LOUIE*
I'm in here now
This happens
I've penetrated
I can't un-penetrate your heart and life
We penetrate
Let me in!!

If you think about getting me out or in… I'm already, always in!
I've entered eternal
You too
We are eternal
Fire, fever, lives
Why get in the way of luminous brilliance
The brilliance of light
Don't turn off the lights
Stop using switches on people
There's no light switch here
Don't switch the experience
There's no light switch for in and now
Now is always in here
I'm in here
I'm always in here

Run around in here and here, here, here, hereby getting it out
There is no divide and separate the truth religion
Dogma
Random, haphazard, gutsy, virile
These live, cowardly hides
Don't hide us
Let us not drop out of sight
Divide, fever, soul, guts
Hear it in passion, in men, women
In weeds are out
I'm not a refugee
Unless you say get out
Take it out of the container
It is here

Get out
Oh, I know you mean it's get out
Unleash it
Let it ride get off the fence of what festers and boils, thrashes, sways, frolics and is flinging
inside of you to be free
What begs and beseeches,
Implores
Ultimately, X-Game-like, explodes inside of you
You know there's more
There's always more
I can't get out of there
There is no 'there' only right here, right now
Man, what thunder pounds and thrusticates and storms through and loves that's giving man
That's giving you
Want me to give?
I know you realize you don't
Realize you realize
Man, I been readin and thinkin and almost livin and you know it ain't enough

Deep down, Come on man, let's deal

Never get rid of it all
So get me
Get me in

Their Son

I was hit
Struck
Standing stiff
Forced to take it
Am I still doing it now?
Thinking the world wants to do to me what my old man did to me
I mean walkin' my whole life
The stiff I was taught to be
I stood there straight, tense fingers, tightened, clenched, clenched, clenched, clenched
Fierce pain starting in my heart
A deep stirring
It was fighting being broken
I would still find ways to love them
But not really
I didn't know it was over
If I was their child, their son—I was
Let's admit it, face it. I was dead
They were dead
It was over
But I didn't know it
I just kept trying out for something to let them back into my heart
But it would never enter my blood again
What flowed though me?
I wouldn't find until I was old
I was a comedian dying for laughs
Dying for acceptance
I was dying every day
But the real me kept dying to live
To really live
See I'm pretty illiterate
But fuck it
I can't get past that little boy

Whenever I am alone lately he stands there stiff
I wish I could give him more
I wish I could give him anything, but I do
When I do comedy
But I'm always mad at myself
Go back, go back and tell them the truth
Tell them what they did
Otherwise you'll always be afraid
In the dark

Target

Asinine sex with the deluded
Wandering-in the land of the lost!
Her big dumb thighs
Her breasts pummeled in her bustier, slash aerobic, girls gone wild, shirt blouse
She sucked on it till she looked like a gay, angry, father, marine, animal
It's amazing one argument at Target with my lovely now, ex-girlfriend and I run into the
forest fire and start grabbing, and humping, burnt, corpse, melting flesh monsters and
tormented, screaming, yelping, tree hangers, simian rodents and fuck the remains of
whatever is twisting in the heat and hot putrid smoke (of traumatized) or I fucked a hooker
and I don't feel good about it

But it did still beat the lamp search at Target

Playa Del Carmen

Long, synthetic, fake, cobblestone walkways
Where a constant flowing, influx of obese surrealists exist
You're not just fat
Fat is ok
Cool
Even cute
But this cartoon existence,
Huge obesity,
Where they roll thunderously to the strategically placed buffets so that you never actually
get to the beach, but you pass out on a piece of sand by the bar with surreal oversized
blender drinks
They stare numbly into your created emptiness
Like I started out with a job and I came out oppressed
Playa Del Carmen, Cancun, Corona commiserating

Comic Hitler

I know man
Look at me
How am I gonna grow?
I mean, I committed hideous crimes against humanity
Now I gotta let women love me for real and I have to get over my narcissism and my sick
rationale and huge ego (gargantuan ego) and sit with her and drink tea?
Hate walks, looks at ducks and feeds them bread
I killed six million Jews
How am I gonna feed a duck
I never gave the Jews food
I mean every time I throw a breadcrumb at a squirrel I think of the tormented Jews
They don't float serenely
They didn't
They can't
I made generations scared and neurotic
That what's I need a plot of hookers
I can't sit with myself and I'm not even talkin' bout how to sit with my own pain that caused
all that pain

TITLE: Action

Journalists are like coke dealers or the errand boys for coke dealers

They pimp you

Try to turn you into republicans

FOX News lies, but every time you go *"I'm not into your lies"* they shove a line of blow under your nostrils

Then when you wake up republican and sick, they should take you for steak like we took the college girl I turned into a new hooker

He reached into my pants and had an asshole pulled out my big cock

My pre-pubescent little cock..

Wandering for acceptance conquering the easy and the hard

Calling it difficult

Making it hard

Instead of just going with flow

The desire

Well, just going with the desire to do the action

Aaahhhhh, the action itself

What a lovely realm

 The action itself

That's life!

My life!

MY LIFE ...

Old Lady

You like that guy
Of course you do
Cause you want to have a few drinks before you can even pretend you find that muppet with
boy band, hair interesting
You know what you should do?
Keep a fifth of tequila in your old lady purse
You 24-year old lady
Cause that's what you are
An old dead thing
Keep a little airplane, mini-bar, bottle of booze in your purse so that you never have to stop
being a robot, with robot responses to that boring guy
Hey, he's cute
Well, he's boring
Oh, here's my booze
Let's see how many drinks I have to do to find him interesting
Oh, yeah, oh!
I'm up to 11 drinks
It used to 2 margaritas

2006

Mink

Why can't my Terror make me laugh?
Do I make my Terror laugh?
Can my terror make me laugh?
Can it?
Come up to me?
Approach me?
And make me laugh?

Terror: "Hey rick Good!! Morning!! Haaa!! Clean? Ya shavin'? Ya shaving and thinking?
Doing the shave and think? Can you shave as fast as the scenarios that speed through
your skulls track?! In and out of the caverns and the nooks, the crevices, where you haven't
learned to give up the crisis—thinking? Can you race your racing mind? Is it a relay race?
Those used to be fun, but frustrating, because you couldn't take all the credit?"

It was a team effort.
You could win races on your own.
Never let up
It's the NASCAR of neurosis.
Thoughts racing.
The Jewish, nervous, we don't fit in, bike race, up and down the chasm and hills, the
mountain of shit—they turned your brain into .
Ride the shit track.

Terror: Hey, Rick what if the audience doesn't laugh.
ohhhhh noooo!!
You might have to go home live in Florida with the old losers and eat cake as they shit
themselves and you...

Mother: I never got a mink coat and that's all I ever wanted—but I gave it all to you.

Rick: NO! No, you didn't. You gave it all to him!! And you!! It's a fuckin' coat!

TERROR

My Father

My jackboot FATHER; Imperialist minded, prole, uber proletarian the most obsequious powerful, huge, little, tap dancing, nigger of a father and his depressed con-artist, sleazy, little, pickpockets, cheap, smoke and mirrors disappearing act, actress of fear induced, fear appearing, anxiety producer (the anxiety family minded, obsessed) with having nothing, safe cracker of a worm, burrowing, dragging her children with her through her infinitely deeper burrowing tunnels, till the earth ,the dirt, would move out of the way deeper tunnels-she made the earth look like it was superficial in its density of shit—she made manure, made sure it couldn't grow anything but more shit, shed, get a swamp actually angry at the lotus flower that could survive and thrive and triumph out of that swamp - so angry she could make a swamp summon and command the insects to tear at and gnaw at the flower for reckoning and redeeming itself from her the swamp. The swamp was a paradise compared to the diseased riddled sewer she helped grow from within her—MOTHER.

The carnal flashes that thrust from her breast and thundering cheerful, enveloped, meshings of her unending continuous hatred of all that ever existed outside her, destruction and constant devastationing devastations.

You were lonely.
You are now defeat!

With what once should have been warm, nurturing soil, turning sunlight, receiving and giving breasts -instead of angry frightened asphyxiators.

Crack whore

Crack whore
Bad morning!
You want political?
I slapped an Asian girl?!
Starbucks sheriff
Incest!
Coffee guy
This girl
It's all good
It's not!
George bush loves when you say "it's all good. It's all good Dude," he says; Another brainwashed, flake wanna-beee.
I wish I could be an asshole, right winger —like in a relationship
One of those manipulative, rightwing, republican, control freaks
If my girlfriend
Sorry, "my honey"
Catches me cheating

Leave it alone
Leave things alone
It was right at the time
It was preemptive against
You cheating on ME
I make the designs
Leave it alone
Learn to leave things alone

On a date we should say things like "Aahhh bullshit, bullshit!"
But I only said, "It's raining"
Ah, bullshit, bullshit, bullshit!!

Look at you so full o shit!

3

There are 3 little boys in side of me
We're not little
We ain't little

I got 3 boys inside of me. I got a million boys inside of me...
I got 1 complex goddamn boy inside of me and he's angry
The other one feels alone
The other one is alone

He shakes and he stammers
To keep people away
He hates them
He thinks the world hurt him
Back then his school did
From his teacher banging his head against the locker
To the older guys mocking him
To Steve L. making fun of him
Steve was never my friend and the old lady made me be friends with him
Steve looked like an annoying, mutant, radiation, mutated, monkey, fetus face....

The *young Rick* in his little leather, dark blue, plastic, cool, pleather jacket:
     What about the rest of us?
     What about ME, man?
     What the fuck about me!!!
     How come you're always...
     Why won't you just listen to me?

Today Rick: These people really can't hurt you any more
     They just can't
     And if things hurt, so what
     That's all they do, is hurt, just that!!
     And I think you should go back to New York
     Who needs these agents!!
     You could be banging all these girls, having fun every night!

Scared boy: Yeah, you're just suffering out here, but in a way I think you are paying
     attention to me. I'm scared and you never let yourself be alone like this. I mean try

for the big stuff and be patient. I mean you've always tried for the big stuff and then you spoke up for Aspen.

See we were left alone a long time to die—even the cool one you still don't know how important he is.

And me (me) the nervous one, you have to figure out how to just let me! I mean I shake so what, soo what. What are you the old man?! My criminal, shit-headed, ignorant, angry, self hating, old man. He wasn't my old man, he was the warden. He didn't even have the balls to be truly psycho, but he was a neurotic, psychotic, asshole.

Now I'm upset.
Why are you so scared to let me, be me?

Rick: Cause you were the one they made fun of, I'm trying to help you and me.

They made fun of you and I don't like them. I'm not aware of the many more people's bullshit, but must it be talked about? What do you think??

That's what they did they all tried to control me by mocking me!!!

I don't call them parents; I call them vehicles of dissatisfaction, dream thwarters.

They watered my capacity for despising and I grew into a needy,
hostile machine with a mask of fiasco

Skewer the Sopranos

Watered down Sopranos
These guys were charismatic charisma
You watched them
You wanted to be them
Like when Springsteen hits his shit hard!
Or writes **the** line
You want to be him
So pure
You wanna be them, him, that's self acceptance
The gangsters I grew up with weren't like the Sopranos at all!
They wouldn't bore you or look depressed, like the Sopranos
With their psychotic charisma
To keep lying
And actually killing people
You have to be bigger than life
You push and push
You are aggressive, to say the least
And put to it mildly – There isn't a term for the kind of physiological motivation, to continue every second as men
Like these

I watched the Sopranos
When they eat a sandwich — **I WOULDN'T WANT THEM IN MY HOUSE**
They're like unemployed or employed delivery men, workin' the graveyard shift
Just punching in and following orders
The gangsters I knew, well you found yourself inviting them into your house

Nothin' bad
It's just that these other men, when they eat it's a hedonistic time bomb
It's a fierce need to keep satisfied
To spend their money on taste and fill up
They always want the best or biggest to feel and to fight
It's so hard to describe
They eat lobster, even deli sandwiches
AND ARE ALWAYS ABOUT FUCK, FIRE AND EXPERIENCE
If they're bored for a second, they lose
They do what they do to live the good life

These are bad men
Men with appetites
They coke it up
Whore it up
When they watch TV, they wonder why TV's are weak
TV shows are weak!
They bet on games
They have to feel like they are the bosses of every game they watch
They size you up and keep looking for angles to enter your world
To impress you
To get you to see them, as someday completely necessary and vital to your home life
Your home

They want to be your bank
Your eventual pimp
Lender and mortgage owner
Even just in your mind
If you desperately need, they get you to think your desperation is part of their solution

They crack open a lobster in a way so you think that they eat better then you and can show
you what you're missing out of life is death
These are old time cowboys who can take over your town
These are murderers and thieves who convince you the minute they walk in, just by smiling
or taking you seriously, that you are grateful at having them as more sincere friends and
confidants
You see, they are more alive than most
They don't slump in their chairs and eat a stupid sandwich
They love the feeling of the gang
When you are with them you feel that these are the powerful men

They emphasize words
When they say 'Sir', it's to confuse, uplift and spit on you
They want to make you feel you are at an expensive resort just when they stop over
They are a dangerous delight
Absolute delight!
You will be delighted at the charm they bring

Not
Typical
Just what's different

And they are different
They make you unwittingly feel that you are part of the world's lie, at what you believe status
is while they delight in your lifestyle
When they are out of the city, they are in your house, in Jersey
Parked the stretch in your driveway
It's because you matter
You are the special ones
The select absolutely selected
You think they wanna know for a second that your dull life is moralistically the real choice
They just scammed companies and individuals
They just took cash from a dead man and are being chased and questioned by the
disgusted FEDs.
They need you
Make sure that disgust doesn't exist
Just charm, delight and life!
Skewer the Sopranos

I envy YOU

I envy YOU for your successes and your failures
YOU got married for your 3rd time?
And you're getting divorced again?
YOU surf?
YOU have the ability to play golf, to have fun?
To just talk to someone
You're never in pain?
When you're sure it's meaningless to YOU?
YOU don't panic?
When YOU do it's no big deal?
YOU don't have my so-called father's voice in your head?
YOU don't hate everyone?
YOU don't need everyone?
YOU don't watch yourself every second?
YOU don't stutter?
YOU like pizza? And that's a meal for YOU?
YOU can still eat fast-food drive thru takeout burgers?!!
YOU don't need more and more adrenaline rushes, more and more sex with different people every second?
YOU do? And you're fine with it?
YOU don't have relationships!
You're able to have relationships?
YOU don't need to figure out how to get what you want right now?
You're able to get what YOU want right now?
YOU believe in the idea, to sit back and let it come to YOU?
You're able to take action on anything right now?
YOU get things done?
YOU don't have to go to TARGET?
You're able to go to TARGET?
YOU don't listen to people?
"I hate people who hate TARGET but go anyway"; Hypocrites!
YOU don't need a unifying philosophy?
You're not hell-bent on finding one answer? Just one! Where is it? ONE FUCKING ANSWER!!
YOU don't get confused by scared people who can't admit they hate? They hate their lives and think YOU need medication
YOU don't sit in your car all day, parked, thinking it's better and smarter to not go into anywhere and just sit in your car for hours parked?

I envy YOU for your successes and your failures

Oh

Start slower
String of pearls round your neck
Who gave it to ya?
Oh, not me
Was it him?
Oh, why worry?
Oh, who cares?
Now you'll be coming back to my part of town
With respect
Oh, thank you
Oh
Two by four
Watch your face
Oh, you left a few things at MY place
Like your eye and a piece of your tongue
Shouldn't bite it when wood is flung
Oh, bad slice
Don't think twice
Can't anyway cause your dead

SCARED AND SCARRED:

The table of the defeated

All I wanted was to get a slice
All I wanted was a cool chick
All I wanted was to play ball
All I wanted was to read
All I wanted was to write poems
All I wanted was to be independent
All I wanted was to play in the dirt.
All I wanted was a dirt bike, knives, fires, bonfires and tattoos

You made me tired and sick
Unending self scrutiny and fear of success and failures, wild impulsive self-controlling fear
of mistakes
Watching myself, anxious, frightened and fucking bullshit
SCARED AND SCARRED
But you couldn't let me do that any of those things
You had to scare me out of it
Scrutinize me, hyper, over extreme, unending
Scrutinizing me
Scrutinizing me to the point of murdering myself
To the point of non-existence
ME!
Not existing?
Not existing!

If I'm such a loser, how come moths are always at MY window?
Trying to get in to my house?
Banging against it
Crashing up against it
Flailing, desperately like out of control wild lovers
They got wings they can fly
Fly!
Anywhere
Thrust
Full-speed

Into the night winds
 And have wild flings and share adventurous nights and days, unending flying streams of passion
They wait outside for me to open the window of my so called "loser room"
Well I call it that
Waiting for me to open the window so they can climb in and ravage me and take me
These moths

I want to walk down the boardwalk in my faded torn jeans and boots
I want to step into the sand
I want to eat her ass while wearing seventies shirts

I was with this guy at this table...
The table of the defeated
Comic: The fucking defeated God damn it! Goooooddddddaaaaammmmmmmiiiiiiittttttt!!
I was at the table of the defeated!

He had this dark, deadness in his face
His veins were drained of all of it – all of it!
I ain't kidding man and I got sick from being there..
From choking on his shit
His fake, strained, stupid smile—that look of pain-people-confuse-smile
They try to blur themselves to blur our awareness of them.
Like these attractive drunks we're all supposed to feel sorry for all these people, instead of fucking running from them running and knowing 11,000 percent for sure, certain, all knowing omnipotent that we don't need them at all ever!
EVER!
11,00 percent.
Yeah!! Yeah!!!
And it's a great feeling, triumphant. But is it we or me who is not?.
You trust this triumphant feeling, these all these stirring-fiercely-spinnin-feeling, these whirly winds of confidence, of triumph, of never needing them again!

So instead, I put on my fixed, fake, strained, look of pain, disgust, hidden, and twisted into fucking bloody stupid, compassion for all these; 'The Katy's' and 'The Daniela's'
Instead I choked on my stupid steak at the stupid football bar
Reverting to your nothing
Without the chief petty officer, owner of the Walmart, do the right thing establishment!
Dull, foggy, green Sunday, death-knell restaurant
I choked on my steak and they had to do the Heimlich Maneuver, twice

All wanted to do was yell while choking
"THAT GUY'S LYING!"
There's a liar at my fucking table
Worse, he's defeated before he steps out the door
He wants to be defeated
He wants it to **ALL** be over
And me, I know the triumph of working harder and harder to be myself to not try hard to be myself anymore—buts its hard fucking work!

Comic: You ever hang out with someone who is defeated and doesn't even want to know anything about himself? That he's just this loser trying to come off like a good man? Phony! So phony that the more he tries look together, that you can only start choking on your steak and as the wait staff team tries Heimlich on ya, all you're thinking as your coughing, you say as you puke/choke:

He's a liar!

The Dog

He has that fucking look on his face
Like a dog that's locked into how people are
He's loyal
He's an organically loyal dog who cocks his head, or maybe his pupils can even dilate when
he is disturbed and concerned by your sudden change in mood
He's like a golden retriever or pound dog
More like the pure bred, obese, chubby, excruciatingly loved golden retriever.
Or pit bull that doesn't want to be a so-called tight ass locked loaded pit-bull
He's always ready, but with a great personality
He's ready to play, even though he's supposed to want to fight
He is an expressive dogface

The Tour

Just back from my empty and loneliness tour
The 'I Don't Like You But I'll Fuck You,' tour
Because my ex ain't gonna put me in the coffin of marriage
Tragedy is comedy's unending seminar

I had to follow a ukulele player last night
Alright I'll admit it
I couldn't get on because of ukulele player

They were booked up because of the ukulele player and the old guitarist who played with
Zappa and who said while testing, while playing and during singing – said "can you guys
hear me ok" and he was, you know, like, the guy who sits at the kitchen table with nothing to
do—FAT

Then the guy who was seventy singing the words to the Godfather theme song and actually
thought the laughing meant they got him.

They really and find me sexy and cute and manly

Soft skin strangers

Come on, Man
You can have, should have gotten have all kinds of women
Fat ones
Fat excited ones
Enthusiastic partiers
To sit on your lap and let you suck their tits and kiss their back and put your head between their legs
Skinny older ones
Ones neurotic about their youth and so they feel you doing things to them is right…
Their soft blonde asses
Soft skin strangers
Women who make like they know you
You can walk into friend's apartments and they fall in love with you
They fantasize about you as you speak and you leave the apartment fantasizing about them.

Joke, They Said...

I'm not good at taking no for an answer
I mean, I used to back off but now I don't
And I've hung in there, what. forever?
No, eternally, really
I'm the white guy with disorders

They told me I couldn't support myself—"The-there-was-no-hope-for-guy"
Like me I went on welfare with the hot modely girl, who wouldn't go out with me?
Just cause she just started seeing this male model bartender with his own useless, male model, theatre group

Of course
So therefore, **A CUTEY PIE-FAKE FACE-IDIOT SMILER-ANTI-PRETTY BOY WASN'T SUPPOSED TO MAKE OUT WITH HER AGAIN.**

"But I'm thinking about you and I don't know why", she had to ask "what does that mean?"

It means you like someone for deeper reasons and of course she fell in love with me

I had to call her a robot, hypnotized by pop culture zombie a few times

Of course she fell in love with me

So I got the hot chick when she said this can't happen again

Man, it did
She fell in love
Got her
When they said you can't rob the Jewish mafia especially if the Colombian drug dealers are sharing the profits
I did
They said they'll kill you if they find out
You'll be killed
They found out
A few fake tears from this once innocent face
No kill
I lived

They said a straight guy can't hustle fags, gay men
I did
I had to fantasize about every woman that ever lived
Put tits on every object around tables
Even my grandmother's arm fat
Whatever went through my mind
They said "you can't just let me blow ya—eventually you got to fuck or be fucked, bro!"
No
I just hugged 'em, more fake tears
Got what I needed and ran

See...
I DIDN'T TAKE THEIR NO FOR AN ANSWER

You have no job experience and your forty
Got a minimum wage job
You can do comedy this way
I influenced a generation
Oh, they won't admit it
Some do

But they don't give welfare to white guys
Got on welfare
You won't survive the insanity of your family
I did

Have a car and an apartment
You're not mainstream
Got an HBO show
They'll keep you as the retarded neighbor
They're letting me breakout
Riff
Come up with my own stuff
You need to do this when the Benjamin's show
Gimme a break!!
Never!!!
Never
Ohh man, what a sycophant!

Pained Expression

I'm so narcissistic that I would be superhero 'Narcissistic Man.'
If you robbed me
I'd be like, oh you can rob me, I'm not even thinking of you
Oh someone shot me, No!

> *No!*
> *I've been shot*
> *Hey, cool wound*
> *WOW*
> *I look like Pacino in 'Serpcio'*
> *Sean Penn in at 'Close Range.'*
> *Harrison Ford in every stupid movie he's ever done*

Oh, I should stop by a bar where my ex-girlfriend works and stand around, wounded
It looks cool, yeah, yeah
I'll tell her I interfered in drug sting stakeout thing
I stopped a gang war or a robbery in bodega and rescued children from a fire and then just bumped into her
"Hey, I ain't goin to no hospital. No. No. No."
"Oh, thanks for sewing me up and yeah alright you can blow me again if you insist."
I love this whole wounded look on my face, No!
This wounded worse than others grimace
Pained expression

Duck joke

You're right
Ducks do walk away from me
I've always been out just for me
Sex instead of love
If you loved me
I burned you
I even feel safer in your rejection
But I'm trying to change
I want to let people in
It's just that they seem so hypnotized by pop culture
See, I've had to be alone
And I've had it kind of rough
You know all those misdiagnoses
The disorders
The hot temper
Unable to get jobs
You don't have duck job interviews
I was the un-hirable white guy on welfare and if you ever seen a white guy on welfare, well, that's pretty scary for those times
I guess you see unemployed white guys all the time
Who else would take the time to feed you?
But you ever stop to see the pain?
You see, you guys don't have the street life
No duck gutter
No duck ghetto
No duck hood
I mean, it's like food
Food, just floats right under your cute little asses
Like, there is a God for you

I mean now
I got money and let me tell you something even having money sucks
You guys don't have to go into stores and look at those shopping assholes or talk to lawyers or business managers who hate their job

Go! Go! Fly to Florida when it gets too hard and cold in the city!
Spoiled babies, you probably run this town
You're worse than the Jews

I'm sorry, I guess I'm racist
But why can't people just give up religion and be good to each other?
Why can't we throw food at each other or dollar bills, in fact here!
Here!
Take some money, see what good it does to you!
You don't have to deal with airlines
Jet fuckin' blue
No just spread your wings!
You should be feeding us!
Selfish foul beings!

The lithium years

Every Jew's a stereotype
Every old lady's a stereotype to you
Every black guy's a stereotype
I'm telling you
Every chick out there is a stereotype
There's nothing
It's over
Every person says what he or she thinks:
    "Their type..."
We have no independent thinking
It's like those dating shows on TV
You see how stupid those people are
They've stopped thinking
They make-out and drink
Probably people watching this are thinking, "hey, make-out and drink," what's the problem
what that? Chill out, passion boy
What is this with the irate, jealous, spectator
It's the lithium years
Take it easy

Drunk

Come on
Stagger with me
Stagger with me!
Like this
Look, I'm an athlete
I'm a jock
I'm...
Do you listen to people?

Come on
Yeah, at least get a wine-o, homeless woman
Oh, man they kiss great!
Oh, when you lie in the gutter
Looking up at the stars
That'll never be yours to appreciate
And you're constantly hungry
And all you can eat is what people give you
And all they give you is shit
Kiss this demented lost, lonely, yuppie or dude with money
And let his desperation meet yours!!

When two people who've gone into the depths of this world are leaving me by the roadside
and are making out while some failure who can't admit he's a failure walks by you
Innerly pouts franticly quotes
There's no greater match in the world
Well, actually there is
I mean you think there is
See, when a garbage dump meets a garbage dump and they kiss and there's no feeling of 'get her out'
We just understand more and more of how this world doesn't matter

See but love, is well, yours
In the shit and piss
Jack Daniels in your pants
Crooked
Moving
Wall

Fucked up SPRINT World

Come on man, you want these idiots to be your bosses?
I mean, "bosses!"
More constructive
And we will hate each other but we will build through it?

Drunk
I'm yours
Losing your thought pattern
That's why I forget the understanding and the pattern
Stay bombed and alone
Not wasted
Bombed
No toasted
Bombed
Well, drugs too! TOO
Take the edge OFF the unavoidable death
But really
Wander into donut shops and get kicked out

Come on
Don't you wanna get kicked out of every place?
(swings arms like flailin monster windmill)
Who wants to be accepted into these places!

What ya need is a good woman!!
Oh, God, kill me, already
Already I'm dead, already
Already is a yuppie word, a mediocre, coping word
I must have been calm and coping at some point of my life
But I can't remember when — ahhhhh!!!
It's all a lie anyway
(drunk slur)
They didn't love you
Whispers
Desperately
They didn't love you

2007

Wilds

Wilds of sands
Salt
Flat Death Valley
This lunar waste howling
Wilds kick up some dust in this brush
Howl boy howl
Wastelands
Desolation
Dessert sands

Singing Christmas Tree

Is the stress getting to you in this desolate, vacuum, country of dry winds banging against
and stinging the mouse's ears, fragile boy
You don't even know me
The government doesn't even know me!
I spread my pussy for money
I am a valedictorian
You do
But how could you?!
You're so compassionate and warm and loving
Suicidal gym teacher and a piano teacher who had anger management issues
Can we all talk about the word faith?!!!
Where's the singing Christmas tree?
When you read the news, act like social workers in a nursing home
I think women should strip
You ever watch the Police Academy movies?
Oh my God, did he just fuckin' say that?

Good Coffee

Why do you ignore what's in your head?
There are winning thoughts in there
Tell people to keep their word
Tell the truth
I'm telling you man
People are hungry for it
Hungry, starving
Who cares about the ones who have to stay protected?
They're meaningless
Less than that
More negative
Down and out!

I can't love you
I mean, I can't love the way you fucking think
I really can't love
Oh, he really can't
He loves cockroaches

My old man was too sick, too envious of me
He was the jealous, the most jealous monster
So I can't love
He wanted me dead
This I fucking know!
And he was bi-sexual and denied both urges
He cheated and lied every single day
So that's what I did and those are the people that are killing me now
When I keep my mouth shut, when my oral, my mustang speech and freeing words and
verbal explosions of connection explode but/and are released and released more and more
and always
YOU keep it in you
Play guitar hero, you play X-box
 I'll talk about it!

I did it
I did it without any of you
Without any of you
Ha Ha Ha. Oh, Mannnn

If I could do everything alone, **it would be the shit!**
Get everything on my own!
I wouldn't need to listen to anybody's bullshit
Preset, conventional, pre-recorded, implanted by other chicken shits who can't live thoughts or words
Mouthings
You fucking parrots!
You fucking parrots!!

Hey, I went to college, now I have a degree
I know you have degree in not having your own thoughts
You have a degree in losing your instincts
Killing them
You have a degree in "In action"
You did a thousand year thesis on how to lose yourself in alienation of your power from your power, you're ability to just be you
Fucking stupid parrots!

You don't have to do this again
You don't have to kill and steal money
You can ask!
You have a great creative mind – Come!
Yeah, what am I gonna do? Invent giant rabbits talking and coming to fucking conclusions of- some sort/type?

Make movie with me in it. "How you fall in love"
Rick: *I don't wanna fall in love. Women are too amazing when they are sexually striving for that orgasm. When they are responding to my fist in there asses. Their bodies. They reveal other things about themselves. They reveal what it is to be a woman, a real woman without the masks!!*

Uma: Try to meet me. Write a part for me as a cop !!! As a junkie. As a poet.

Rick: *What are you writing? I have no interesting talks with anyone, really I wanna see what you're doing, on your own your private, woman cove. Your cove. I wanna be in your cove – not date and hear yer bland, given-and-take, hear, and no - thinking responses - conventional, pseudo, responding, **RESPONSES.** Tell me it's a fucking poem!!*

Is it lyrics?
We should talk in lyrics all day, every second long!
I don't want to hear
I want to look
I just had a talk and she told me about her condominium
Who is she?
Robot-like robot
Altruistically helping the big fuckin' fuck!!!
Come on
Show me
Take me into your fucking individual landscape
Your psyche
Make it, Man
Make it a different world
For me right now!!
Now!! Now!! Now!!

Hi honey
Sorry I'm late
You look nice
Was it expensive?
Is the coffee good here?

Mother Who Went To Palestine

I went to Palestine and dealt with the peace process
I figured it out and I did it
I took all the rocks and I replaced them with little rubber balls
Oh, they're having such a good time now
They stopped with the name calling which to me is worse than suicide bombing
Oh and err uh, I replaced those terrible bombings with St. Johns wart and organic free range oranges
Apparently, this is better than suicide bombs
And everyone is telling each other, '*ohh look at this orange… Look at that one* '
Hey, they the sky is blue
Why bomb each other?
I'll never be able to eat an orange like this
Even though refuges don't really have access to oranges much less to internet
I said, *'don't call yourselves refuges'*
You're road runners
Now search!!
Google a makeshift tent!!
Go!
Refuge, Shmefuge
I said you're lucky
You have an outside to ehh, live in
Some people don't even have an outside!

Explaining photos guy: Fallujah

Look.

We were taking pictures and they wanted to be in them and I tried to tell them "You guys! We're taking pics of the palace and you know we ain't never been to Iraq so we want the buildings, the mountains, and all the beautiful places, we, uh, er, uh, bombed." They wouldn't listen and they ran out to get their clothes and just fell all over each other. Well, we just had to get this shot and they started goofing around.

Hey, look at me with a leash on
Hey look I'm a killer Doberman, "ruff, ruff"
We make better human pyramids then you
Our wrestling team is better than yours
We play naked S&M Iraqi twister, better then you do
They called one of our soldiers a dyke so a fight broke out that's why you see all the bruises
I mean name calling?!
The porno vids
We partied a lil' too much

You Know, *'Iraqis Gone Wild'*
'Reservists gone wild'

And by we, I mean YOU

Cop At Bank: Helping

Cop hears, "Why am I helping them?"
I'm getting something done that will change your complacency
Your pet is complacent
Your complacent life
You pet it
Feed it shitty pet food that he don't tell you is garbage
But as long as your complacency eats a little from the cute can-that looks concerned about your pet Complacency. Healthy, complacency food for your pet
Complacency. Healthy, complacency treats
And don't say "oh I get it"
Complacency as metaphor
It's complacency it lives, mopes around, doesn't live, mopes around as seemingly as a controlled pet in your house
It stands, hang-dog, head drooping and not knowing anything, any more except that it is ignored
What is this freaky fuckin' speech!!!!

These are real thoughts as opposed to you 'getting it'
Let's create art
Art ain't art if it's called art

Why should I protect them, they stay small?
They won't deal
 Why do I have to be the one to help them keep their lives small?
>   Well, wouldn't you hate the Jews too if you had Jews taking Jewish chunks out of
>   your paycheck?
Don't stare ... you might see!!!

Cop: You are too tentative. That's the problem. Watch out for that
Ya get so tentative
Ya start to get numb
Ya stand fuckin' still
Ya walk from A to B and back again, the rest of your days
Take the gun and force it into her fuckkkin psycheee... There. There!!!
Now you think she's gonna do anything?
Tell her she's got 2 seconds not 3, 2!! 2!!!
And she's gonna do nothin' but what she is told to fuckin do

Whatever she had, all her other agreements will be dissolved, destroyed in flash
There's yer money, now go!!!

See people gotta care about their community
People
None of youz cares
You sit and you wait for it to be over, like yer fuckin lives!!!-
Like!!! Yerrrr fuckinn n livesss!!
So youz are all dead in the water
So you don't have to be killed
Hey you get up!
Get up right now and try something!
See I had to tell ya but here's two hundred fer not getting' and lookin' confused
First you had an instinct, just do it — Ya trusted it!
God, this world makes me sick
Don't it make you sick?

A Butt for YOU?

Why should I give you a cigarette?
All you ever do is nothing and worse you don't create a change
You just sit and get stuffed
Stuffed as chicks
You are stuffed chicks
Your are stuffed frozen stupefied, petrified chicks
   Hey Johnny, come over here and look at these petrified stuffed chickens
Chicks, your chicken chicks
You been told what to do and you do it
I'd rather give a homeless guy a butt
Why you?
You're really the homeless
He has a home life
You kill life and create life-less-ness

I mean, what have you ever done?
I bought these
Not for people like you
What have you ever done?
What will you do, worse?
Ohh, man your gonna make worse shit outta shit!
   Merry Chrstmas, Happy New Year!
You didn't say anything
Proof!
You do only to repeat
You repeat only
You say and do nothing!
Repeaters
Stop the repeaters
The constant perpetuation of repeattin-repeaters!
Killing 'em
You repeat?!!!
Bang!!!
Now!!!
You don't!!!
I cured
Where you are right now?

No, you cannot have a cigarette

Scratch 'N Sniff

I scratch 'n sniff tats
That's all America is to me
One big scratch n sniff
 I scratch all day at the layers of people, the postcards they've become
- — The self promotion
- — The ambition
- — The unmet needs

I want to sniff out what's wrong with society
What can I do about it?
Type shit?
But it always leads up to the big guns
The people in charge
The stuffed suits, stuffed with how to live by bribing
Stuffed with greed and big bank accts
AT OUR EXPENSES, TYPE SHIT
I can't arrest them
I NEED TO BE ROBINHOOD
That's truly what I need to be
But for whom?
For what?
For these people, I give to the poor
Who?
What?
They don't stand up for themselves
What's that?
Why that?
I don't want to steal form anyone
I want to arrest the situation
Punish them
Stop them
Get others to rise up
That it?!
I type shit?

Comic: *I've seen you guys with the unmet needs. I sniff. I sniff and sniff to see where the truth is and there is no truth anymore, anywhere*

Ever

No truth

The Fight

I lose sleep starring at my gun
I get up each morning and in the middle of the night, with my heart racing, beating hard or at
least I can hear my heart beat
I don't ignore it
It doesn't ignore me
Nothing ignores me
The war, the facts, the fact that you need protection!
The fact of how you look at me and even if you resent or hate me or judge me, you also feel
safe knowing I'm right here and that's what I am.
Right here.
I'm not having a sandwich at home
I'm not at home
I'm here
But you just want to believe commercials and strippers and thug videos and bling and shit
All you want to do is show off and call it 'keepin' it real'
You what's real?
The love you won't let yourself feel for the aged, the sick, the scared, and the poor
The victims
The victims are the kids, the ones who will never ever be educated
I wasn't!
I was slapped away from myself
I was not educated
This is all I could do with how much I can care for things; Values, my own, not religious or
republican or my own what exists right now
But I don't want my values anymore
I want toothless hookers freshly showered in my bed!!!
I want booze all over my body from nonstop drinking' and cocaine
Lying to women
Killing my parents
I want to kill you if I feel like it because you have become idiots
Let your children grow up friendless and parentless
Let 'em play sports but teach 'em how athletes are the ones with no values
They let their values be taken away by the scumbag agents and corporations
See, I want to fight for you
To really be alive not just to exist as robots and the brain washed
But there's nothing to protect
You are all George Bush

But if I stop protecting I become him and Dick Cheney too!
The bum boy, fags, wimps in chicken suits

I Saw a Lot of Pussy Last Night

I saw a lot of pussy last night
A lot
I love the pole climbers at strip clubs
Sometimes I think I get the stripper thing
I did more with them then normal people who put on sweaters and behave
I don't want to get to know them!
MySpace is proof of that
I like this band and that show
It tells me you sit around while other people create
I'm bored
I sit around and wait to say stupid things on an eventually cancelled TV show about
having a family and a wife and kid and relating
We shouldn't relate
We should not relate
WE SHOULD SIT IN ROOMS LIKE NEUROTIC, EXPERIMENTAL, MONKEYS
AND PEOPLE SHOULD JUST THROW THEIR ARMS AROUND US OR LIFT
THEIR SHIRTS AND THROW THEIR TITS IN OUR FACE
Why talk?
We're all lost and stupid any way.
Look, I'm narcissistic
So don't even try
Unless you have the life force and passion of Che Guevara, what are you gonna tell me?
How great my space is?
How addictive?
Your either gonna be hateful of Republicans, or actually defend them
Hey, people need to get off the dole
It's become a welfare state
"Welfare helped me!"
Let the rich politicians give back the money they earned
No! They worked hard for their write-offs and expert loophole lawyers
They should be able to keep their mansions and bank accounts
While we believe the lie of what's right and wrong

My girlfriend

I think it was like trying to turn me into a ski instructor...
You put the white turtleneck on me and the Christmas ski snow sweater
I went and got the best skis
The shiniest and toughest for the hardest slope of this relationship
I'm at the top of the huge hill
I realize it's cold wet and dull and gray out
And then I realize that skiing is the most uninteresting sport in the world
So I'm going into the cabin and sit and think
This ain't me
I'm turning into the blonde, ok, boyfriend
I'm going to watch strippers and never be involved with the uninvolving again
I think I want to be the wild, ranting, homeless person
I was one!
And I just want to walk around saying "there's no God and Republicans are murderers and you're all shit!"
But then I think how I used to sit with her and pet the cat for a second
I say "I had a life"
Then I realize, I hated it

All relationships have led to Whole Foods

All relationships have lead to Whole Foods
That's when you know you're in a serious relationship and have a good job
You're at Whole Foods
In the middle of Whole Foods
Pretending, you're not a moronic neurotic
Looking at loofahs and goat's soap
Free range losers, who can't handle the fact they are eventually gonna get sick and die
> *No, I'm not*
> *No, I'm not—cause I throw away my pants each day*

They say never wear your pants from yesterday, *its old energy*
Always buy organic hemp pants and you can smoke it instead of using chemicals to clean them
> *Because having stains on your pants means having stains on your chakra/auras and*
> *a stained aura blocks goodness in your life*

The goodness is blocked so you have to smoke it and you'll feel so much better
> *Hey! I need kale. I need kale and free range chicken*
> *Uhmm do you have milk free milk and meat free meat and manless man and*
> *womanless woman, passionless passion*

I have a passion for goodness
Only organic free range goodness
Then the chicken dies in a good way so I can eat it
> *Not eat, digest*
> *Not eat*
> *I don't eat*
> *I put it into my body*
> *Eating is so abusive*
> *I never eat*
> *I watch what I put into my body*

Soy

I'm angry at Starbucks drinkers buying into that corporate crap
I just want to get the Starbucks customers mad so they get disgusted with themselves
And I don't have to wait on a long line

The Vagina: It became America's Heartland

It's this the vagina, the silken cavern that calls to me
I call it America's heartland
Cause of the rusty bulldozer and the half built mineshafts...

NY

I'm so lonely
I always need something
So I want things
But I'm afraid to go outside
It's good to be in NY again where people walk and mean shit
They don't do the 'float and pose' like they have nothing to ground them
Narcissism isn't grounding
There are people in the world but in, LA NOBODY CARES

Paycheck

Here is a personality that has been developed by TV
It's small, tiny and stupid
TV is over!
Unless you wanna watch James Woods or Vincent D'Onofrio or Tony Lapaglia act like male actor heroes
The personality, the overall mannered, mannerism
The mannerism people, they suck
This sucks, what's happening in our society
Nobody has balls as comedians and they just want to get in, get in, get in!
But I don't know what to do to get it bigger and bigger and bigger and bigger
To stop being liked
To challenge people to go beyond challenging them

RESPECT

Here's the thing I just saw
This old black lady from first class with a stupid wig
She thinks that her get-up gets her respect?
You're supposed to not stare and respect people?
But they have to earn your respect
What if they don't get my respect because they're mice
You are taught to respect people
> *"I am respectable. I have a big fat wife and we walk slow-weee wallk in our sweaters
> and jackets REAL SLOWLY my friend"*

"I eat the shit of the man, so you who look and act different are to respect me - The oppressed micey mouse!"

Angels piss me off

Yeah, you out hang out by the 7-11 not the Quzinos
They are all yuppies at the Baja Fresh
All them dumb girls who get cars from their parents
But the at the 7-11, all them are thrashers
I'll tell ya who's doing it and what's going down next
Right before they vomit

So you wanna blame me?
I couldn't be a good dad the government was always spying on me and making it impossible
to get my food stamps and having to look for work while on the check

Angels on a cloud
There was angels on a cloud and they was telling me to visit my daughter and get
something
Food or something
There was angels sitting on a cloud and they was telling me...
They was talking to me
Talking to me to be a good man, otherwise I was gonna be in trouble

You assholes don't want to hear the truth
There was angels and they came upon me, ME!
You fucker pigs, You!!
I hesitate to use the word 'sin' on ya, but I will fuck you up, fagots

You sit around here smiling and getting along and live mildly
But the angels told me I had to better get along with you all and I mean ALL
Every single one of you!!
The angel walked up to my face and told me that he talked and he fucking said it to me, MY
face
But I don't want to get along with you and I have no interest in what an angel tells me at all
Why would I want to listen to an angel?
Bitch-fag-soft-angel
I'm me, not some angel's sensibility

Angels piss me off
Like they're always right
Who says angels are always right?

Already I mean, they're walking-invisible-uppity
They got all the answers because some rich lady with connections writes a book about
angels and then Oprah, Donahue, whoever, gets to paid to hustle it
Then we listen to angels; like them books about McCain in Vietnam
He's still an idiot writer without the water torture

I been tortured
Ex-wives, kids, family businesses... All my life not just two years in Vietnam
Playground, school, walking to school ditchin' and serpentine-ing, in and out
Not showing up cause of the enemies in America
I face every second, every second in this country
These American enemies
People who judge me
People who hold my money back?
That's the new people – the enemies
Who hijacked my money back and tell me the rules and believe the rules
Like idiots, fucking useless idiots

God?
Women?
Also because good wise arguments without any logic
He pouts and cries I'm good, I'm God!!!
I'm God
There are no answers, there's just how you want to live
Better yet, there's just what you want to do
How about how you are, what you want to be?

She Wants

Then there's Angela
The true criminal
Just walks in to stupid situations but turns them into brilliant landmarks
Like the Twin Towers of Stupidity
She shows you why it's wrong and so right
She got involved
She'll fuck you on the floor because you bore her and she'll show you the stupid things you
say the stupid things you say will run like the psychotic demons
 The dumb rabid dogs of thought they are
Through your stupid design of stupidity, your house
See because you design stupid things just to get her
Your life style and all she wants is, what she knows she wants

If there were a God he would have designed it that way
Ya gotta get is what you know
Ya love fuckin' chocolate or making fun of people or creating huge symbols that you've all
come to represent?
If she gives ya smirk
The you're a jerk-twitch
You ain't even got the power to make her do anything but shake your bacon strip of a spine
You've been porked out of your power
You little anemic pig
She'll try to give you a shot but you'll turn it into the 'I can't keep up with her. Why does she
make me realize I lie?' And then you'll forget you lie and she'll inch a little over
What snitch you oughta be
Your only calling is heard in the yelp of your 'I don't exist-ness'
She walks away

You'll know she's gone but your life won't change but you'll ignore your hunch that your life
could've gotten better because, 'how could that be?'
She must be like most women but why do the lice start crawling all over?
It's ok, I can still ignore the lice that are me. ME
Why do I miss her, she's just a chick?
I got plenty of them
Ha ha, look at how stupid I am
I'll call it smart and I'll forget she was ever here

It's the only way I know

I'm gonna keep it clean
Ok, but we can't talk about comedy anymore
Here's to the short run cause you ain't gonna be here for the long run
So sell it and wonder why nobody cares and the ones who talk like they do, don't matter.
Ever
Hey, here's your check
Wow, now I can buy something

All that one wanted was a fuckin' house
All this one all wanted was behavior and to be desired
Sydney all she wanted was to have me shut the fuck up
Claire wanted incense and weed and sleep pills and ten minutes of sex
I guess that's a fuckin' life style
Hey, you're cute
Let's get involved and share spiritual books

Laura

Gimme the criminals any day
Instead of the ones fittin' in, stay in' unhappy
Fittin' in
Suckin' up
She was
Gotta
Amble
So slow,
So thick
You won't even know it's a gamble rollin' more than yer dick
Her eyes like slow, slippin' snakes
Slidin'
Approachin'
Starin' you through
Yer eyes burrowin' into your heart
That's the hard part
Oh easy to let her go, but then you'll never know where her true love makin' can hit ya, lead
ya, throw ya
When she lets you in it's even more, more
It's even prettier

Call me

Oh yeah
The safe and loved circus carnival of Eros carnival of the phone call!
Carnivals of keepin' high
Keeping my head from losin' it
Dance so he don't do the insane asylum in his slippers shuffle, ohhh!
Oh, of course and don't think about how rich you were and busy and then how everybody in comedy knew
Show to live
Except you
HEY!
Hey, here's one for ya
How come everybody enjoys life but you?
Oh, go on MySpace
Live it up!
Live it up!!
Come on rock the world
Kick ass on fucking MySpace

Come on twisted-balloon animal-psycho-happy clown-cutie-gummy bear-bubblegum-sweetart slut, with that mojito fittin' philosophy

Think I'd ever hang around a priest that was fuckin me?
People don't know in this country to walk away
 Ideal-lies people
Know if you see priest dick ya walk away
We're America

Machine gun girl

Wake up drunk
Fall down and think about me
Am I absolutely haunting?
Am I absolutely haunting?

You're so in the moment
Is that what patriots say when you tell 'em they don't have to be for a country but they can
be for their own individual life and points of view!
I'm not just hot
I'm what hot really is, but the heat can't stand
So I stay out of my OWN kitchen

> *Girl: Ya know and I make out with men I think I can control*
> *Other heated up men calling me hot but I go out with the ones who won't hurt me or*
> *tell me what to do but he don't do anything that does anything*

Machine gun cute girl who could a been hot, interesting life bitch.
Now, I'm not a woman.
I'm a woman who will wake up a miserable 35-year old, talking about how they ruin chicken
fingers girl and call dead, dull, boring bands great. HIGH FIVE YO DUDE BRO

> *Hey yer cute and don't you walk out on me*
> *Hmm, I pretend to play the control game*
> *I'm uhh, yer hot*
> *But I don't play or control anything and games are kinda creepy, and the ones that*
> *make you feel excited, excited, excited fade – HI, umm yer boring, I know I can*
> *control … you wanna go hear this great band*

Angela : You need hold my machine gun, Baby. You need to fire. You need to fire
something. You need to make something hot happen around ya.

See Rick knows a girl who uses her guns is the answer

Obsessive thinking

I confess, I confess, I confess
I gotta confess something
I gotta confess something
I gotta confess something

Chain smoker: We Gotta Get Outta Here. We Gotta Get Outtta Here. We Gotta Get Outta Here

Don't obsess so much. Have a drink, like me and look at me. I get along with everybody, People

What does that other guy gotta confess to, we already know he was a prostitute

Rick: And the women, the trapped feeling, the wasted time, the trying to be a good boy

You are your own authority

I'm your needle honey
I'm your best nightmare
If you can make this guy work for ya
You'll, we'll have...
A tremendous three weeks
Writhe in the aftermath of pain
Blame me for everything and get bored by any guy with the ability to love you calmly
I do for you and desperately miss my narcissism while you lie ultimately alone not
appreciating the sweet waters of sweet waters of a good man
See, because I know it's adventure you want
So any time you want to travel on the lost highway the heart of darkness ...
My apocalyptic gun boat awaits you

Guarantees

Yeah, yeah!
I like that
Guarantees
That's what this world needs
More guarantees!

Come on!
Bush ripped the country from us
He lies
Cheats
Murders ...
For what he and only HE wants

We are Bush's bank account
We're his disposable cash and his fucking assets
What we have are his assets and his investment cash!
Cheney walks through us
Lying to us
Taking without one redeemable act
Anne Coulter is becoming a sex symbol
Nicole Simpson and Paris Hilton are articles of interest
Interesting now that we have become bland sheep

I say get very drunk
Tell the people in the entertainment industry that they are cowards
Do you think I wanna talk to you?
You gave up buddy
You do jokes about fish sticks man
You do jokes about your fucking laundry
Say "Bitches," white boy
Say, "ho"
You think I wanna talk to a stupid manager?!
You think I wanna ignore what's going on in this world?
Everybody's fucking programmed!

I wish I got blown by my teacher or I wish I got blown by my priest then I could be forced to
turn gay!
I don't know what I want, man!

I don't know anything except I want pussy and I want drugs and I want out!!
You want in man, IN!
You wanted to win!
Am I the disillusioned man, Man?
It's all stupid
I can't get in if I'm not 'dumbed-down' into a mini man-gargantuan-idiot-seized, guarantee

Not your man

I'm not your man
Get me away from your plans
I'll burn your idiot scams
You don't see that I don't need to be who you think you need us each to be
I'm a schizophrenic
Incorrectly called that since I won't take your shit, at all
I'll talk to myself 'til you walk away with thoughts that there's nothing left to say
You don't even know that you live that way
Every day
Never, nothing to ever say
You ain't just white, your white noise

New Rap

I'm a liar
See my dick it's on fire
I should explain it because you can't sustain it
Flat butt
Thinking it might lead you to do something different than just blinking
U like a horse sniffing himself
That's you, You!
Like corpse that's still sniffing glue
Your balls sitting on the shelf
What I need 'em for never use 'em
I want in
I'm a fitter-inner
I'm just a loser call myself a winner
My friends all agree
My friends all agree
We just nod our heads like haunted house ride and we the fake dead

Timing

A guy talks to me about timing
It's all about timing
He has no mind
No fierce thoughts
He doesn't trust the men of passion
He fears it
No real wants except safety
So he has timing
He is boring at great lengths of time
Continuously times
His expressions of no self
Just have fun
"The guy who fears fun"
It's all theory and manners and about... "Come on man take me with ya"
Better yet buddy!
Buddy!
Budddyyy!

Yeah yeah!! You're my buddy you always take me around
No, you always leave me home!
And go out be the big-bad-go-getter!
Go get, but can't you take me with ya?
Can I wear my cool guy outfit? Put a bed robe on, with my hair all dirty?... Come onnnnn
what's with this shower and shave stuff and what's with this having to be attracted to good
looking chicks or anybody and what with having to d more than drink coffee and smoking
why can't we drink?

Why can't we just run around asking why?
Why!
What's with errands baby?
What's with Staples and Kinkos and going on the internet and reading the news and
MySpace shit-headed-ness?

Come on man...
Look how cool I am in my open robe
Yer dick hung out on national TV and you did a skill that you can stop now
You can stop
Stop now

I taught him that
I'm what they ordered, gave him
As for the father, I'm what the fucking lord gave ya
> *Young man, have you had the appropriate check-up, asshole?*
> *Yer an ssshole*
> *I never told you that I think you and all people are assholes*
> *Ya blue collar bumm ya buuuuummm!*

God why couldn't we all be dead instead of having to deal with you and having to look at
you
I'm an adventure!
The go-getters, you better, you better –
Piles-o-shit with the stench of ambition
Look at you, look at you!
What if I was never impressed
Like beaten man who actually wins ever day the prize
Here you are
It's you

Talking: An Abstract part of the body

It doesn't matter
I'm not worth speaking up anyway and when I do it's always the wrong time and taken
wrong and no one understands anyway and everyone
Well the truth is I'm waiting for someone to save my life and I worry too much about what
people think and then I get beaten down again

I want to be bad
I'm sick of things being good for me
       We're helping you
       It matters so much
       Were putting your work up we here for you
       We taught you how to be good
It all makes me sick and bored and stupid
What is this grateful shit
Why does anyone ever, ever, have to be thankful for what somebody else did for him
Why, why, why
I was a cop because I chose to be a cop
I choose to be wild comedian
I choose to like cockroaches and hate people

Monsters

Nothing but monsters
Eww, awful monsters!
Mean monsters, who aren't even mean
They are invisible
They aren't even that, if the are invisible it means
They do not exist
They never existed
They've never ever existed, not once
Not for one second!

Monsters do not exist except for politicians and famous people
Monsters, eww, *'I'm the monster of Rick'*
Not having what he wants
I'm the monster of your daddy
The daddy monster
He was never your daddy
He was a sick little fuck
A useless, unnecessary little fuck
Sick fuck
They aren't monsters, they are little men
The monster ambition
The greed monster
The monster AA
The Monster, *oh I cannot think!!*

George Bush is Lying

George Bush is lying
Does he have a to-do list?
9-10, Lie
10 -11, Lie to people and tell them I ain't lying
11 -12, Act like cowboy and twitch and twitter and do real defensive facial expressions
Really defensive ones
Lie about uranium claims
Lie about Hussein
Lie about Osama

Get real mad
Look like a psycho that scares little mouse Americans and let's face it all Americans are little mice men

Mouse man: *I am mouse man, I agree with everything you say!*
    I'll do whatever you tell me
    I'll go where I have to even up your ass
    Into the lose your way by kissing so much ass kiss ass, chute

The idiot video gamers

The new idiot alienated youth
It used to be
Johnny Rotten
Jim Hendrix
Now it's the video pussies and indie boy band and girl poser singers
THAT THE NEW ALIENATED IDIOT WATCHER

MySpace Blogs

Rick Shapiro the Opera!

Ralph Macchio,
Ralph: *I'm tough, I'm sweet, I'm scared, I'm hard… well I'm always hard.*

I'm tired of great audience members and great employees of comedy clubs coming up to me and covertly expressing "I'm what they want to see onstage," "I'm who they love" and "I die laughing when watching" and my most cherished (that keeps me, truly, from going volatile, with a gleam of inner bellowing) "Why the fuck ain't you up there! or when the fuck are you coming to where I live is despairing, disguised as frustrating "when you coming here brother!" And then not trusting themselves to step up, like we all have to in this world especially since it is the way it is now (and secretly always was).

The time for not trusting what you want- whatever you are passionate about… is over, it's ok!
You don't have to say "but what do I now!" or the frustration (in my case angry, shamed, humiliated, Jew fear of the wrath vacuum) of "I'm not an expert." It's over.

Look what's been happening to comedy by people who label themselves "authorities" or the newest innocuous poison of them all: "I'm also a student of comedy." Oh, okay but don't study your fears, don't pound the book of 'you' with your eyes, don't go further. Just study what they tell you, it is and never feel the loss of your own knowing again! Look all over the world, because we sat back because we weren't labeled "authority." The educated ones are just graduated eternal trainees. I got a better education by not ever trusting college. Definitely, the day I left to do what I want, down to the smallest thing, to the vision that was and is ever growing and explodes out of me that was the day the audience members gave me everything. The ones who trusted that their minds were alive and a myriad of their own individual strong thoughts went flying through their minds.

"Aaahhh," said the ones who get 'disgruntled' … "is that even worth being?"

The ones who believes Americans should and must be afraid and proper and stifled and sweating thinking they are threatened, also gave me a lot a shitload of pleasure and absurd, cartoon face, monstrous humor, as well as the ones who gave me their all knowingness, their sense of fun and who they are: Acerbic, irreverent, you know the complexities from skaters (real hot-doggers in life). The Johhnny Knoxville and cronies, Borat and The Guerillas and non-rigid fuck-heads, the ones who have their own smile, smirk and bolts of hurricanes shooting from their hearts and guts out of their eyes!

Tell the bookers! Tell your boss if you work at a club it's time for you to do and get what you really want! So many people stopped going to comedy clubs because of how dull it all is. We need new audience members to speak up! Heckle icon comedy clubs, heckle in churches! Heckle at any food franchise. Demand more! Come to my shows and demand more and demand me and demand more of me! The world has activists in it, don't label yourself 'active' or 'inactive.' Enjoy yourself and your passions. Kick ass with all of who you are. I love my audience members and I love the ones who hate me. It all stirs hate, love and humor in me. Go baby go! Come to my shows.

The Meek Shall Inherit The Meekness

If you do cartwheels do 'em outside of class, outside of fucking boring appropriate (you're so appropriate) America. DO 'em while you are waiting for your pancakes at IHOP, down the aisle. You are a nice-trained, trained to false, smile, Miss America, pleasing the old men with her false anti-true girl ways. Miss America is not the way any girl would ever choose to act ever. So buy into it.

So you have to buy more to keep buying into it. "Hey Miss America, right wingers and liberals lost their homes." Can you talk about that you pumped up, pump up, on pumps? Miss America, gay marriage ain't the issue. Life is! I mean Miss California, USA and all the girls who believe they should be dead and others should be if they ain't the moldy molds of the molded moles.

If you do back flips do 'em on yer way to the table at complacent restaurants. Our environments are too mannered, keeping us small and dull-respecting the respectfully false altruistic "he's a nice guy." Nice guys... Real nice guys inspire, they aren't "nice," they aren't dulled "respecting the respectfully, false altruistic and meek." Oh, wait to be seated? Oh, four empty tables? But wait to be seated? Stand here, only hear now, grumble at me? This table free but wait to be seated? Oh, respect people who talk new age truth to me? Oh the universe? Cursing is anti-spiritual? Can you be anti-spiritual? Who is this version? Oh, Obama isn't doing anything? Can you be angry? Isn't it bad?

A guy said to me "can (can) ya be angry that long after explaining to me how the GAP is?" Convenient. Obama isn't doing what he said? No matter what you say. Oh, they want a ghost thing but there's already a ghost script? So make it a zombie thing even though they don't want a zombie thing. Uh, okay, yeah. You saw Harrison Ford in an elevator? Or actually held the door for ya? What other triumphs were there in this life time? Hey let's preach to the converted on the internet...

More in an hour. The specific hard hittin' stuff comin' up!

wakin up in LA...

Wakin' up in LA is like waking up in a vacuum of self hate. The gentle winds of self hate quietly steal…

Here's the thing. I wanna blog. I wanna do this but I can't type and its like pissin' in the fucking wind. You feel more alone when your typing or word-processing and you have to say 'uh oh, spell check.' Spell check! I hate LA so much I can't sit behind a fucking monitor. People out here can suck it. They want the stupidest projects to get done. They do the stupidest, not even funny enough or (well, stupid comedy is fucking great)

But they just prove to you they can host or they're attractive but no one knows what it feels like to trust themselves at any cost, any time of the day or night. The cost of not trusting yourself is always a longer, worse payday, in the long run. Get it? If you don't, **YOU BELONG OUT HERE SAYING THINGS LIKE 'IT'S TOO MUCH LIKE GHOSTBUSTERS, SO DO A ZOMBIE THING.'**

This is a giant, lying, dull, dry, vagina. I think I have a bent cock from living out here. Who cares? Blaze… Blaze through all this shit and start speaking up and not like those politico-pseudo activists who really just want fame. Personality is gone from this country everyone just wants to word it right and spell correctly.

terrified mamas boy then he went into see me then he blamed his fear that he already had on me

Ok this man little man, in physicality. Facial expression, don't exist—Brain and testicle sized and he happened to be short and stocky like a Rush Limb-believer, teeny, mal-formed testicle. His chest out said, *"Good show, I was terrified though. I gotta tell ya, you're dark."*

"What's terrifying."
     "Uhh uhhh uhhh uhhh uhhh"

He couldn't answer, see cause it wasn't. He's terrified. People are afraid of searing, searching, able to make themselves able to be heard, over hovering, over the herd hawks! I'm a comedian not a warlord or political hawk or lying politico-ass kiss banker, business. Listen to your use less Mom, fuck! You can't even admit you know your mom is useless and you still take her advice even though you know she's useless. *Moms are useless pin-heads, see Son?*

Rick Shapiro: I was on a plane with a woman and a guy (both Sarah Palins, of the Midwest Sara Palins) talking about lawn bowling! With authority! I don't wanna write right now but she was and he was, they were doing Sarah Palin's authoritative, being there, moron monkey's speech:
     "Hey, ya got a sun roof cover? But what really mad, me fume, (cause that's what phonies do they fume), was the traffic ticket and we went to Vail. Dashed in. Did our decorating. And my daughter's in Human Resources at HBO. She needs to dive into the resource pool and get human. All I know is when I retire … We all sat around the dinner table and actually discussed our favorite sexy movie. Scenes and bridge and other shit.

I can't write, no can do... but don't wanna fuck this corpse shit

la hollywood transplant transplanted muted mutants, what happened to girls and women-robots

I have friends that fear not making money so much it's like talking to people who don't think they exist
To exist is bad
To live worse
To think and feel my truth - uh oh no!

I went to a birthday thing for a friend who's been nice to me and there for me
And the others seem like small men and the women are just girls who don't realize the game their playin is over. They say less than nothing. Their voices demand tiny. And tiny as their choice to use nothing in them is a glaring, self eating, monster, ravenous, rabid, and out of control. It's so sad that it's hard for a thinking man (able to live and use his thoughts) finally, has less than knowing friends. Friends who think they must know they are never allowed to know themselves ever again. "Hey, I hope the empty garage is all you've dreamed of because it is all you've dreamed of," I told one girl.

I asked her male mouse friend "Did she marry a Beverly Hills doctor?

Him: uhh no ..uh yes, actually...

Me: Yeah, I can tell usually with women with voices that high - it means they married someone they hate

Next subject doctors, and also girls who say nothing the rest of their lives

lost my mind halfway thru shit-blog about shitheads

You believe I went out with a girl who wanted to be raped? I know because she started her time with me when I said this booth is good, right? She said, "where ever is fine as long as you help my career."

The first mulch out of that corpse, her mouth, rested dead, hung in the air like a shit covered dead cat hanging off a dumpster. And how about uuuh, the one who shows up wild and acts like Sarah Pailin? Scared? No spell check forcing myself to blog fake stories of me, making friends in shithead alley called 'stiffs told where to turn.'

More later, these were actual moments.

> *I sing in a temple now. I have to respect my parents, you know… How should I market myself?*

> *"Me too, 'singer not anymore chick and bad is true fear monkey, bitch cunt why do you sing for old ladies in pearls?*

No more broke artists!

What the fuck did you just say to me?

uhh heyy

Why would people be so-called, 'satisfied?'
I'll say it.
Walk around dead.
Is this enough to not create, to buy and stare, to buy and work extra jobs? Nobody yells on the street anymore, saying, yelling, what they fucking want. So it's satisfied time now is it?

No! nooooo!

> I had a talk with Jesus and he talked about video games or gaming like the dull gamers call it. Why not walk and think? Let it disturb your lost-ness into seeing. Seeing I ain't lost. I ain't never been lost. Stop now. Get in my way. Get in my way.

How come Sarah Palin can't tell the truth? Because you want to drink mojitos or whatever garbage trend and be a garbage, lipstick, pibfound in gasrbe wiflernv bg bg hbmsbslmrtjt,,n t,,,

I just lost my mind

bye

my hero obama mccain and sara ??Vote cynthia
mckkiney

I'm sick of this shit
I don't know who I am
I know who I am
I got to be proactive
I gotta come up with a clean set but Obama smiles like a 2-yr old. Chest out ass kiss and
McCain has already been deemed the more the fool he is. The more he will be shoved into
our un-fighting faces as the new president. What Obama? Oh yeah, he seems like he's
gonna fight the WTO and really pull'em by their big diseased, corrupt ears and make 'em
face him. He's our hero. Nobody talks about it. I hope they put a bullet through my head but
I have a clean set now so things will be getting better for all of us.

Sara Palin is GI Joe the doll the movie, the cartoon, the tattoo

Cynthia McKinney, ever heard of her? Find out... she's the one

tight ass

Fuck London
Fuck the world
Fuck the forced Frisbee-ers
Fuck the uptight girlfriends
Fuck the politicians

No bring 'em to me and I will show them how the comic's actually discuss them; as though they are affected by the 'white noise'

The whiteness noise of the black man
The whiteness noise disease of the 'hey I'm white and I don't identify, I don't feel like McCain except for the fact that he'll say anything to keep eating his blonde wife's asshole, sucking the diamond shaped shiny shit out of it

We're gonna get the 'over spenders' and the 'me-firsters' out of way
Yeah, start with the trophy. You just bought a $30,000 dress for and her rented leased $280,000 earrings?
You leaser.
You lease yourself, you scumbags!
And tell Obama to stop smiling like six-year old white boy who just showed us his 'A' grades and became class president, while the world, and his Hawaiian middle school mocked him not cause they were assholes but because they saw right through him

NO SSPELL CHECK!

Just sick of the beer gutted actresses, marketing male nurses, dressed in Irish pretty girl garb, who actually say don't want to talk about my job
That's fantastic
Reality?
So let's fantasize
Long story, more later on these poles with brain removal syndrome
Is it the whole world?

And respond with life storming thru your response, please
Clever, useless, dead words, will be buried without a look at the corpses face
Also look up Catherine McKinney if you wanna see black and woman running and fighting together
Green party who cares what the party is

PS: Inside, to a good friend, on fire...

Man the more you hitch up to my ball cuttin by 'Frehd Spa Handbook' the more they shake like readied rattle snakes...-

I'm still lookin!
Found a place for 2 weeks then I'll have all the money move until then there's poodle print on my panties and I'm under the gun of the disoriented Gods that uhhhh disorient me

Throw away the straw and bang it back!
Keep reminding me of that
Hey you know any AA type peeps
I'm not sure it's what I want but I think I gotta go
Too many roller derby, tattooed-babies-snortin and need to, uhhhh, hear the AA shite

vital, faarrtts!!! Lala

Farts
He dances and makes farts
He does
They bring the inner explosions out
Dance, he doesn't shuffle or amble
He explodes
He is the choreography of explosion
What is in the pizza?
The food that sits and burns inside the man
We need to let the explosions out
He regurgitates his inner life
The fart is the dance of explosion
The noise of the body
The man lives
The body dances while we think, feel and live
He explodes
He farts
He resounds
We must all make sound!
Our needs and desires clamor and bellow
They echo deep inside while he dances and lives

bad poetry

A man alone stands in the world with a retreating bone
With nothing but his bone
His heart is dead
He's on fire
His life is on the wire about the world—he's run from
The personals
As he tries to love the real, but images surreal flail and stare and call
Sounds in the now dead gone wind-remain
Where is he?
Where is he?
Where is he?
See I suck at the practical
Hate errands and thought I loved the ones who fight to lose
But that's me
I win in the moment
Where true eyes see no guitar heros really live any more
There are no guitar heroes, so you have to be the one
The non-heroic win
While the big visionaries are taught to be hot dog flippers on the late shift
Beaten down to socialized false security
What country is this?
I'm sick of blaming
At least my heart is flaming
Eyes try so hard not to see but reminded again my eyes are all I have right now
But let the winners keep taming it down

obama???????????????????????????

I have the best news for ya

The world doesn't make sense

I'm always in trouble or I'm one of the few if not the only one, who admits it anyway

What's trouble?

Why do people even mention McCain without murder next to it or we could assassinate him

but let's just watch the murderer

They used to just look like they we're killing our time

Now ere seeing our time is real

This is real time

Pull out of the war

What time?

Not what day!

I want to know

What time?

Look at your watch and make a decision

What a lie my friendships, my life, my beliefs

Obama smiles strong

They make the candidates for the American smile-a-thon lift weights with their teeth

They should have bullets shot through their cheeks to let the air out of their bloated rectal

smiles Implants, aaah no coffee

Go now, to, uuh, coffee

Get it or I got to speak like mice

I mean uhh, who you voting for?

try to figure out how to do it - just got off plane and didn't finish sentences for those of you...

Why did I have a good time at Tuscon?
I keep asking my self
The Hotel Congress, with a great rock club, all young people who look like the trendies in NY but with actual genitals that are heated up by the blow-torch of what idiots call the devil and the powerful religious and is really in actuality, actual, actuality fighting and sex. Not the emo band and these girls are sneaky and hot and they are sneaky in that 'uhh don't bullshit me, confrontational, true enjoyment of way, the way to true enjoyment. Sure they are all tired of their lives but they don't pretend. They are agros with tats of their agro

About to write more...
Listen man, NY is a sleep and stupid and sterile
Unless you know how to fucking deal and steal

Stanhope feels like your finally standing while he's dealing, real dealing, not alternatives. In that 'here's another way to uhh, errr, you know, uhm, enjoy your life if you ain't rich and powerful.' He's saying in the coolest funniest way, fast and more!

There's always mexico; fifty dollar disease killers. While the disease of America expressed by Rick while Christen was showing fun. He made it fun for me. "Shoving a finger up a mad dog's asshole will release its jaws from around your ... " Ya gotta hear him say it, he's only doing it a year but he's not a dullard, emotionless, salesmen, dentist like the ones who want in immediately and suck years later, forever. While America stares into their tourist bag of being tricked and chortle without really looking ever at who's onstage. One cardboard "dude after another" with some exceptions - but Doug and guys coin-up and me, we, exceptional — no spell check and starting to resent.

Can't write today. Stanhope is a riot, a real riot. Comedy's paced and marching like funny uhh, ish: Hand soap salesmen. My heart, my guts, felt alive again. Fighting and fucking.

Can't Sleep

Man, Tucson with last liver and giver
He don't cut his shit short
Man, steaks
Colors, baby colors and his cool hot chick
Like a wind up
And looks ya in the eyes
That's what it was
Doug Stanhope looks at ya and really talks, not like the others
No way!
Comedy
Fighting and fucking and looking off stage in a corner and seeing the shot man look
All I'm sayin, everything... everything —-
While they hold back and suck ass and kiss up in NY, LA and MySpace
Whattya mean, of course?
I had to pay extra
Missed my flight
Lost my paycheck
Who do ya think I am? A guy who hates me!
Oh, I kicked ass too, multi-doug, multi-rick
The new friend Christen and the coolest fans
Trendys with anger, not like the floating floaters in NY on a float
I mean I love my fans
The guys who crack me up and I need to laugh more than everyone
Do and as much as you
Other fighters with no love thrust upon your childhoods
The guys who crack me up are the ones with burning, wasted lives, in their eyes trying to
blame me, smiling at me and screaming in their untouched heads
Ain't slept
Fuck anybody's need for goddamn coherence
I want real unstoppable coherence
Oh, oh, it's up to me that thing
Oh, okay coherence and incoherence

What is any of it?
Of course I lost my cash

rape of 2 tails

Rape the wash insiders
Don't climb on top
Jump
Hit 'em with clubs and 2x4s in the curve of their self protecting, curving backs
Wash insiders
Those are just the interns "the ....let 'em know how we feel by the rapes of our bank
account, cigarettes and cigarette money, gas and religion and —there's more something so
much deeper but got to uh, smoke
I'm so bored with the fact that rape is fun
If it's not really rape, right?
RIGHT?

Better yet

Let's always joke around in diners
It makes the hard workers and people who gotta stand around all day laugh
Do-it because of the yuppies on the upper east side have no sense of humor
The elevator was down so "we were all waiting, a long unhappy 3 seconds" from their apartments
Frowns in navy blue everything
I had my zebra trucker hat on
And I said (out loud—on the upper east side where banter is about babies or tiny dogs, cause they are the only one with impulses and moving any part of their personalities) I said out loud to the standing corpses "must be one hot elevator" they looked at me and looked back

Now I know why I hate the 'so-called adults' who scoff at dreams
Freedom and the truly fighting to be proactive
Better yet mentally alive!
Better yet...

Blue Suit Sale At Walmart

Can these blue suited, hiding their hunch backs, lizards?

These hamsters, steak eating porterhouse, living hamsters?

Obama and Hilary and McCain force themselves not to blink so they look like X-Men and they are X-Men

But they reverse the meaning by staring into the non-existing Lord-in-the-sky to fool and tweak and make giddy, the slow moving obese farmer

Strong farmers now reduced to Walmart, wall starrers

Roses and guns

Oil is the money shot in our bukkakai-ized, jizz-thickened, homeless street whores

Extra $400 if we keep our mouths shut and thank and thank and thank them and hollah

Blue Suit Sale at Walmart

why pounds through my head like thunder disguised as a friendly knock

I grew up with or actually against a so-called 'pop'
With long legs as literary imposters
Say an imposing figure
Why are the literary so encased in safe cliché they call 'description'
Also ain't no fucking spell fixins here
I wish I were a dolphin then I could pretend I'm lookin at ya
I know but do they really see us and why am I so afraid, even when I know I'm not or is it think
I'm not-materialism?
It's so funny, isn't it?
Hey look at this lamp
Hey honey we have enough to invest in a hot dog right now
A ceramic, imported, well-designed, meaningless-weenie
Everything in most peeps houses are meaningless
Oh, that's why I'm always tense and afraid
I don't run enough errands (that's true though—espesccially since its mere phone calls)
Mere was placed here out of laziness
Mere is not for the 99 percentile to think there the 99 percentile
Why is comedy so stupid
And there the big money ones, why?
Pounds through my head like friendly knock on the door that is being forced open by the thrusting assault of the inside barrage of 'whys' that will break the door down to let the 'whys' fly
Not like Harry, Disney, pothead idiots
The 'whys' demand and demand
But I wave 'em off with cigarette ashes
Like a sad burnt Mom who failed with her kids and smokes Bensons and stares blinklessly at her beauty-less lawn

words like snow in a paperweight - ahh the crystalline
forest

Hey let's pretend were dirty vs. clean
Hey let's make sure the audience is brought in
Hey let's not realize they're as strong willed as us
Hey lets smile at the seven million dollar dullard
Hey let's not care what dullard really means
Hey let's watch our exes think they're so happy then wonder why they're so wasted-
Well at least they're happy
I make 'em miserable
I scare homeboys cause I don't act like a regulated white boy
But the real homeboys get it, see it and the real blacks get it and the cool whiteys and the
smart whites… Shit man, they all get it
Some just don't want to face differences and enjoy 'em

"what up"

I'm sick of hypocrites

I'm sick of my own hypocrisy as a good man or a loving guy

I don't care about your cappucinos

The enemy is people who think they are so fucking right because they follow and believe
the structures in the skulls, built up by years of sitting and hanging with family and meals
with the secretly hated

I don't care about the life styles of the wannabes and the proud and stupid newly developed
so called successful or on their way

wild pilgrim

In Whales they were like waiting for a very nice meal and then I came out after the politey's did their over-dinner-acts

The audience was like a pile of expensive, unused, silverware with some cool dudes and some chicks who got it

But the other side of me saw that they were into it

Surprised

Oh, is that ok in comedy to surprise
Shock their brains

hate blowjobs - love the neighbors

I was talking to this hard core pornstar
She loves to fuck
Okay, America
Ya ever ask yourself if you love to fuck?
Or do ya just like it and sometimes, need it?

And she said how her mother and her were driving

Later in blog I describe how someone asked me to close the blinds before I fuck her. Why? I don't want the neighbors to see. Why not? Who says they care and if they do let 'em. Also they are across the street! Also, Why? Why? What's yer point? About not wanting someone to see? What is your point? The neighbors. The neighbors shouldn't see. What's yer point in this life. "I don't want the neighbors to see." Do you ever ask yourself what your shame is (what lie you buy)?

Hey here's a Jesus statue
What lie do you buy?
Your judgement of the whole surroundings that you're creating
No spell check
I'll fix it later
It's like the blowjob, when the girl says 'I'll do it to make you happy"
Why not do what you want and really confront yourself on why you do it?
To make someone happy? Why do you hate, hate, hate sucking cock?
Ya ever see the excited porn star suck cock?
You ever see someone who gets cock, gets blowjobs, gets sex, gets satiation?
Ya ever see someone who doesn't??!!

Let's not be excited America
Let's deal with right and wrong and talk about Kramer and Dane Cook

not men

These LA fags
Guys who suck dick or ass fuck other guys
These ain't fags
Those are just guys who suck dick or ass fuck other guys
I'm thinking about—real fags!
Guys in there faggy cars who think their fucking cars are what make them interesting or fuckable by those fagot girls who actually get?
Okay, what fucking the fag cause of his faggy mobile, that he should be hanging from?
These fag hangout, fags, who fag around and fag their careers up and fag out all over you during their fagot conversations.
Hey, Rick I want the testarossa
Just like you so we can get back at our exes

Rick: *I wasn't saying that. I can't care about the car. I never even said anything about a car much less a fuckin fag testarossa. FAG!*

Hey people are people, Rick

Rick: *What are you a faggot? Fag! (I couldn't use any more words I exhausted every have of verbiage and linguistic contortions to raise the level of conversation, the potential even for heated discourse sunk and decayed to a pile of non-metal manure spurting slowly and morosely from this guy's toilet skull).*

I'm talking about your fucking corrupt mayor and also that fagot ordering his fagot eggs, like a faggot posin' his poser-ness around, like the fag he is. I'm sick of these faggy wanna-bees and hanger-ons. What happened to men and women out here? They just hang like limp transparent shit shirts.

Hey, I'm a blouse, fuck me, see how I hang!

devil definition: lawyers

Lawyers are the only thing that defines devil
With their lower lips hanging
That lawyer lower-lip hang, as they hang people
They rise up from the manure piles stored in hell and spiral through the earth
Drill with their devil screw to screw you
Drain into your bank account to drain your bank account

little survey minds - take your stumbling in the dogshit of your mental waste somewhere else

Little survey minds

Take your stumbling in the dog shit of your mental waste somewhere else

What's it like to be brain dead?

Really!

Little survey sheep

You bother me with your little brained, small minded surveys

Have the balls to "fuck-request" if you have no true burning or courage inside you

Your needy little survey begging shows

What tiny scrambling, stupid, distraction monkeys you are

Hey, look at me

"Like me"

Maybe, Fuck me!

Waaah!!!

I'm an idiot

Like you

When we gonna hang dawg-bro, kid dude-girl

I rest my case

Each instant, the stupid responses from the ones who need to be accepted into the suckling suction of the "keep'em stupid" tank of fearful homogenizing and fitting in and lazy no thinking, cute boy girl, emptiness

They will spread in the diseased corrosive comments they shit outta there little limping "wanna-be" heads

Got a call from someone who has accomplished huge things by hanging in there with the truth-n heroin way of not listening to the ones dying by dying to fit in

I'm too sick of you stupid survey, baby monkey shit-headed, sheep herd, shit-to do, spell check or rewrite for dickhead coherence needing "fun li'l posers"

So chill out peeps (while you really chill away… watch)

Cool! Yo

Off the chain, Yo

I like chillin' and basically, you know, meeting and greeting, the new... Right?!

Yo??!!

heroes!!!!Get a self

Why do you have heroes?
Aren't you the guy who has to wake up every morning and make your own decisions?
Aren't you the guy who walks out that door and decides to look someone in the eye and ask
them for something or demand and wait?
Wait for their answer?
Aren't we the people who act and wait?
Or act and get?
Don't we have our own days and nights?
The heroes?
Aren't there?
During my days and nights, that I live and survive every second
When I put my hand on that doorknob and turn it, it's my hand
Not your hero's
My hand, my body goes through that space, that I opened up
I've learned to hate some people, thanks to reading their MySpace
The only word I could believe, shit-scum-delusional
Their wanting to sound cute, idiocies
So I'm not gonna idolize this guy or that guy I'm gonna talk to you
Or
I'll just talk to me
If I talk to you it ain't gonna be just talk

he's cute, so he thinks he's funny, cause I say he's cute -
monkey paris hilton wannabee loser chick

Me: Wow, he felt? Felt it was important?

Other me: Yeah, he likes what I wrote

Me: I'm not going to encourage you, I'm gonna kill you, make sure you always hate yourself

Okay you want a blog here's a blog
I'm sick of comics thinking they're so attractive with their short fagot ass hair and their I'm
edgy but I'm fitting in philosophy. Also too bored with emails and blogs and MySpace for
spell check.
I'm sick of how comics walk around because idiot chicks say, "he's cute" and the guy thinks
he's funny because some lame, brain dead, pink bloused, sheep, gold purse, pink Paris
Hilton brain, wannabeee says "he's hot" so he thinks he's funny when the dumber he is the
more the reality show, white chick talking hip-hop idiot says "oh, okay I guess he's funny
because he's uhmm, he um, he looks like uh cute er something.

When will the idiots die?

They won't?

Where are the snipers!

The fuckin ...

i also pet cats, get lonely and i have a killer smile, i'm
cute!!! I swearrrr!!!!

Republicans,
I don't call 'em that
I call 'em what they are... Predators
I call 'em what they are... Terrorists.
Democrats, I dont call 'em that, I call 'em what they are... Republicans
Or frightened, sweaty, anxiety, riddled, grandmas in khakis dressed as men, that's what all
politicians are.
Ewww I'm frightened of gay men!
Ewww I'm frightened of poor people!
Ewww I'm frightened of sick people!
Ewww I'm frightened of anyone who wasn't born with a shiny shit eatin' smile
I'm frightened of people who don't own shiny shit or shit shiny shit!
Or talk shiny shit!
Politicians are shiny shit
Shittin' all over everything

suicide bombers-i don't call em that, i call em what they are — starving—broke

Suicide bombers
I don't call 'em that
I call 'em what they are... Starving, broke

They have suicide bombers
We have homicide bombers
Both do it because they're broke
When I was starving I tried religious fanatsizm
I know why am I 'being' like this on MySpace?
Let's talk about our "favorite" shit.
Why don't people get real interests?
> *Oh, I hate reality shows, don't you?!"*
> *Some are cool, dude, right, yo?*
> *"Bring it. Bring it. Bring it"*
> *"Yo - how – bout - a - lap - dance – ho?"*
And say 'bi-atch' a lot when you email me!

I'm a bad poet

I'm a bad poet or I'm a real bad poet
I jump on cars till we're against a wall
Somewhere
Somewhere in a stall
Somewhere
Somewhere
You know where we are?
You know?
Yeah, shit this place regards me holds me in high regard
Oh, look at her as she's lifting, pulling off her shirt
Get the description
Only if you get it right
I'm walking around now
I'm alone as always
The cold wind
The dark
The street
The cars light it up
I can see but feeling has to become impossible
It absolutely must be never possible for now
Forever is what I thought gotta find
Someone gotta be outta their mind
Breathe Baudelaire
Always be drunk
Ah, I get it now but I write
Always be outta breath
Damn man
Shoulda made that sorter more effective
Always be drunk
Baudelair, me?

Always be outta breath!

I'm the guy who wrote Parking Lot Love!

Simple nighttime romance

I create open

I'm running now

She's coming now

I had no idea she could read as it were

As the reasonables say 'man gotta study that false idea'

That phony way of reasoning man!

They keep telling me I'm crazy, ha!

I'm here man, gotta keep it together

That thought

Gotta keep it together

Ha, man oh where's that place?

Ah, sat with it here a few minutes

Oh she's kissing me so righteously

I thought righteous was for the religion robots

Now it's for her kisses

Oh, man. Am I a robot?

I don't feel like one

I certainly absolutely don't look or talk as if I were one, Sir

Ah, oh!

Shit look at her

God she's so beautiful in this stall, her ass tattoo like a theme park direction

Sing, ohhh

Her skin

No theme park a girl!

A woman intelligent slutty?

No dead word

She's girly girl girl girl and breathes and flows like the woman

A woman

A mystery

Man, oh another

Oh her little tough, sweet teenier girl arm reaching behind for my cock

Can you?

Man.

Oh her little vagina

She just flowed, brooked and coined her way around the best

Now her arms, oh!

Look at her arms

Reaching up to hold the stall wall, the top so I can ravish

Meaning lick and kiss and suck and taste

Oh baby you're so bad

Oh, you look so sweet and little when you're eating and getting

Being bad

You're so honest

When you're bad

Oh God, you're such a real little girl

Such a good little girl

Oh, you're bad

Shit

Back up to the streets

Sessions

Trained by the Taliban

I'M TRAINED
I'M TRAINED
I'M TRAINED BY THE TALIBAN
RUN ROUND TOWN
BOMB IN MY GOWN
HOLY TOLEDO
NAIL BOMB TUXEDO
ISLAM IS DA BOMB!
VIRGINS ON THE BRAIN
TALIBAN TRAINED
I BELIEVE YOU
I'LL RELIEVE YOU
I'M BIGGER THAN THE PRINCE O' PEACE
HUGE IN PARADISE
ROLLED THE DICE
CAME UP CRAZY EYES
WANT MINE
NO MORE TIME
BOOM BOOM, BABY, BOOM BOOM!

All the Girls I've Never Wanted

I wish you could have heard me. I wish you could have heard the lies, alright, my lies, as in, "I lied to you," because it was you in the room, all and each of you!

Dammit why'd you let me live my unlived life.
Why'd you do that to me?
Why?
No one needs to be lied to, to be allowed to lie like that. I told you I was trained to not ever wants to not ever want what I wanted. Those wants occurred in me like an abused child's fairy tale.

These burnings, these flames, the poetry, the Dickensonian lyrical images floated by fake expressions, warped, twisted, hate exploding hostile scowls passed over these whims as I thought they were impossible **UNHAPPENINGS**

ANTI-WORLDS THAT COULD HAVE BEEN

I was burned
Babies
Burned for you were extremely wonderfilled, feminine — human theme-parks, water splashes – but for the other boys, you were, we were, bridges away. To far away holy lands' dogmatic manifestations from the organized sewage constructs, the stench rising methodically; expert devil shits climbing, seeping into the humanity of then unheard beauteous children of million-colored flaming, floating, flouricides combined, from hopeful for us.

Realms, kingdoms, king-deemed, doomed, these middle class Dickensonians eventually heard the bell of eventually instant Nostradamus dropping from broken ropes, pulling the absolute lonely bells of seeming finality.

Destination arrived but now to leap off the mountain of the undesired life 'n fly away from the whilrling *"How did this happen?"*

If he can have, why can't I? Eyes, heart racing is a and only important once distant now exploding color-filled self!

The Australian from the Pink Pony. Me, finally onstage, expressing rage at all the ones I knew as beauty, therefore not allowed to lick 'n notice with my own now-alive organ, the paint brush reaching – like only a paint brush feels 'n taking the other ones THE OTHER ONES WHILE LOOKING THROUGH SIDE EYES AT HER, ONE TIME I WISED UP – THE GIRL WITH THE BELT 'N BANGS I CALLED IMMEDIATELY – WOW, HOW DID THAT OCCUR, OH, BY ME

THE… the Amsterdam girl, tall in beauty not so, though ohhhhh man!

'N Terice, sooooo lovely 'n cuuuuute, me turned off though 'n the stripper who massaged me the night I cheated on the brilliant Terice

Dee from the beach totally hidden by her shame, the scummy villain chieftain, odd grafters smarmy in its warmth, cold reality ignored on the walk home with denial saunter.

Dee, Allison – not loop – more to come

Next the girls I wanted.

Grim Suits

GRIM GUYS IN GRIM SUITS BEIN' ALL GRIMMMMMM 'N SUITY. GRIMMY 'N
SSSSSSUITTTTY.

HE DID IT. IT'S LEGAL. LOOK AT LEGAL, ALL GRIM 'N DISAPPOINTEDLY
GRIMMMMLY DISAPPOINTEDLY GRIMMMY DISAPPOINTEDLY. ALL IT'S HIS
FAULTILY. ALL WE'RE GONNA GET AWAY WITH-ITEDLY 'N LOOK AT THE SENATE
LIKE, "HEY WE PAID FOR YOUR ELECTION-LY LIKE HEYYY WE DIDN'T JUST HELP
YOU WE MONEYED YOU."

 THE GRIM SUITS LOOKIN' AT THE OTHER DEPARTMENT O' GRIM SUITS. THE
OTHER DEPARTMENT O' GRIM SUITS LOOKIN' AT THE OTHER DEPARTMENT O'
GRIM SUITS. I FIGURED IT OUT: THE DUMB PSYCHO REPORTERS CALL IT GRIM.
IT'S COVERT. WE PAY FOR YOUR HOUSE 'N VACATIONS 'N LOSER KID'S
EDUCATION 'N REHABS.

 WE KEEP – YEAH – THIS IS LIKE WE KEEP YOUR SECRETS. YEAH, DON'T WORRY,
THE COVERT EXTREMELY INTENSELY SERIOUS "WE" KEEP YOUR SECRETS. YOU
KEEP OURS 'N HEY! YOU GUYS IN THAT DEPARTMENT, WE, THESE TWO OTHER
DEPARTMENTS KEEP YOUR SECRETS TOOOO.

DON'T WORRY, LET'S ALL – THE GRIM – LET'S ALL JUST DO THE BLAMIN' GAMIN' O'
KEEP THE BLAME DOG 'N BLAME COVERT WE KEEP YOUR PONY SECRETS GAME
'N SMOKE BLAME THEM SMOKEY MIRROR OF IT'S UHHHH THAT DEPARTMENT'S
FAULT WHILE WE GRAB THE LOOPHOLE 'N EVERYONE LETS IT BLOW OVER WITH
A CELEBRITY ALL OF A SUDDEN BEING A WIFEBEATER OR HORNY OR RAPIST
OR...

HEY, LOOK, TIGER WOODS' BALLS...

HEY, TMZ SAYS THIS CELEBRITY IS UHHHHH... OK!

Someone Simple

ALL I WANT IS SOMEONE SIMPLE. YOU KNOW, SHE PULLS HER HEAD OFF A TABLE, RAMBLES ABOUT FRENCH EXISTENTIALISM. I SAY, "WHAT?" 'N SHE SAYS, "GUNS 'N COKE." RAMBLES ABOUT.

ALL I WANT IS SOMEONE WHO KNOWS, REALLY KNOWS 'N TRUSTS 'N KNOWS, I MEAN TRULY GETS 'N SEES, 'N REVELES, LUXURIATES IN THE TRIUMPHANT RESOUNDING BECKONINGS FROM DEEP WITHIN. BELLOWS CAUSING RAPTUROUS, FEROCIOUS, VIOLENT SELF-KNOWING THAT HER MOUTH IS HOT!!! 'N HER MIND MAKES IT MOVE!

I KNOW, I THOUGHT THIS WAS ABOUT A BLOWJOB WHEN I STARTED WRITING THIS PIECE. IT'S DEFINITELY, ABSOLUTELY ABOUT THE BLOW JOB EXPERIENCE, 'N BALZAKIAN [BALZAC?], DESADE, SAMUEL L JACKSON, STIEGER, JOURNEY.

BUT IT TURNS OUT IT'S ABOUT HER BEAUTIOUS CONSTANT TRIUMPH THAT LIVES 'N LIVES MORE 'N UNENDINGLY IN HER MIND AND BODY BABY BODY BABY BANG BANG BANG! BANG!! BANG!! BOOM BOOM MIND 'N BODY! THERE SHE GOES WALKIN' BY! BANG BANG! HERE SHE IS TALKING TO ME! BOOM! ME! BABY BANG BANG! DON'T KNOW WHAT TO DO, JUST LISTEN MAN 'N FEEL THE FIREWORKS OF IMAGES LIVIN' YER LIFE FOR YOU! THE RUMBLE O' THE ENGINE, HER FACE, THOSE LEGS TELL HER WHAT YOU KNOW!

STOP THINKIN'. IT'S THOUGHT. THAT AIN'T THINKIN' 'N IT'S ON THE OTHER SIDE O' LIVIN'! YOU KNOW, IN THE DUMPSTER, BUT YOU CAN STAY IN THE DUMPSTER.

YOU WANT THAT OR YOU WANT HER LIPS ON YOU 'N YER HANDS STROKIN' HER SKIN, HER HIPS, HER ASSSSSS OHHHH MANNNN BE A MANNNNNN, BE A...

BOY HER EYES! TORMENT CAN'T SUCK YER COCK OR LOOK AT YOU LIKE SHE CAN.

IT CAN'T RESPONNNNND!

These Blue-Suited Creepy Crawlies

These blue-suited creepy-crawlies. These scum-swilling gum-to-gum, their mouths keeping the scum rolling their lies around the roof of their mouth under the tongue, UNDER THE SCUM-LICKING TONGUE. These men, hah! These women, hah! Hah! Now I know it's simple, unless you're a person who NEEDS, CRAVES, WANTS to be lied to and NEEDS, WANTS AND CRAVES knowing that he's being lied to so he can sound smart. Hah! Smart.

SMART! When he says, "Oh yeah, they all lie. Yeah, but they've been doing that for centuries. Oh, it started in the Roosevelt era. Oh it ended and started and ended and started with the Revolutionary Reagan Civil Warian Cuban Overtake Era. When I was in *that* good college. Did you know Lincoln had a beard? Hah! Smart!"

Yeah, we know you know they lie and that they've been doing that for centuries. I mean, we see a so-called MAN, or as I like to call 'em, LIZARDS, that were taught and trained to wave and show teeth and so mastered imbuing ever-so-perfect combo-like threat and flash at terror with Christmas lights. These blue-blazered neon signs saying, "We've been doing it for years," and we see this man or woman, they were born as these. And they wave. We must know that a blue blazer means destruction.

> Give me a guy that is too busy to give speeches. A guy who says, "Huh? Oh, ok, here's what's goin' on. I mean, EXACTLY what's goin' on," as he makes a speech. "Vacation? No, I'm giving a speech. $20,000 dresses for my wife? Not 'til their wives can... and what kinda loser wants that shit anyway? Lemme get this straight... the economy... $20,000 dress. 37 cent raise for the minimum wage... $20,000 dress. Appearances... 37 cent raise for the minimum wage. No thanks, I'm not a scumbag. "And get these corporations out of my office, god those guys are fat.: blubbering, bloated, and broiled in their boiling... Get them outta my office, outta OUR fuckin' White House! And you know what, bring those protesters in here. I wanna hear what they gotta say. Well they're guaranteed to be, at least, much more interesting than fat, blubberin', scotch-swillin', porterhouse-lobster eaters! God, they don't fuckin' stop! Nothin'! Nothin' comes outta their mouths.
>
> "'My yacht! Took a lot of hookers!'

"'My yacht! Took a lot of product to buy my new wife!'

"'My yacht and my wife,' God! GOD!

"'The best hookers are in Bali.' Fuck! FUCK!

"Who cares?!? I gotta listen to this shit?

"'Golf course in Dubai.'

"I hope we're shippin' AKs in that area to somebody with a bandana or a cowboy zapatista uniform. Anybody but a suit! No more blue suits! God, God. GOD. GOD!!!

"Fuck! Here comes a B.P. guy. Look at his bloated, greasy, smirk. I gotta say hi to him?

"Hi Bob. What's that on your chin? Destroyed fisherman chum or a piece of a boat? Did you answer that email about who's responsible?

"God, GOD!

"Oh yeah, she really loves ya, I get it. She's a mistress but she really loves ya. I get it. People are all corruptible, I know.

"WHAT?! WHAT'D YOU JUST SAY?! SO, WHAT'D YOU JUST SAY?! WHAT'D YOU JUST FUCKIN' SAY TO ME?! PEOPLE ARE ALL CORRUPTIBLE?! THAT'S IT, FUCK THAT, FUCK THIS GUY!

"I love choking CEOs. GOD, Jesus Christ and Allah, I love choking CEOs.

"Hey, let's put that in our speech, you fuckin' speechwriters. Let's even come up with a how-to book.

"Look at this… this is on TV, right?… Look at his face, my fellow Americans, his face turns redder than when he heats up, when he laughs hard with those disgusting guffaws when he screams out rationale, like, 'It's survival of the fittest, hahahaha,'

"My fellow Americans, look at his face when being choked. It looks the same when he yells, after six Scotches, 'And some people are just bad luckers, Bob. Right, Bob? Right, Bob?'

"'AND IT'S THE LION VERSUS THE TURTLE, LUCK OF THE FUCKIN' DRAW!!'

And now the President is throttling the CEO, "You wouldn't be LUCKY if people had access to, not money, not opportunities, the SAME opportunities, not funding, no not that subsidy shit, no, not any of that shit, Bob. BOB!

"Your throat. If they had access to your festering, boiling, fat-puke, corporation, puke-bile-broiling, bile-burning throat. To your throat.

"I, as President of these United States, hereby give each and every human in this global economy the throat of this CEO, Bob In Bobsuit, and the complete freedom of anyone to throttle, no CHOKE. Here are the keys to the throat. Every first of the month, a throat will come in the mail...NO, BOB DON'T WAIT FOR NOTHIN', HERE!! WAITING? WAITING? THAT DOESN'T EXIST FOR CEO THROAT. THAT DOESN'T EXIST FOR CEO THROAT! SO, FROM NOW ON THE CITIZEN CAN CHOKE AT WILL!!

"OKAY, [STAMP], IT'S DONE. CHOKE WHEN YOU WANT!

"LESS GOVERNMENT REGULATION!!!"

GLIB MAN

GLIB MAN and RICK are at a fancy dark restaurant with thick, elongated wooden tables, high ceilings and raised booths.

> **GLIB MAN**
> Hi, I am Glib Man. I speak very glibly, very easily. Oh... Oh... The government is awful. They are totally ripping us off!

> **RICK**
> "Do you think there's anything you can do about it," Glib Man?

> **GLIB MAN**
> Oh, I thought you meant *ISSUES*, you know, have a talk... my point being... what time is it? Could you excuse me for a second?

time passes...

> **GLIB MAN**
> I would order the dolphin, but aren't they an endangered species? But why do they protect dolphins? They are smart and used in science, to learn communication with others. And they beat them on the heads.

> **RICK**
> No no no, that is seals.

> **GM**
> Baby seals, that's right.

> **RICK**
> Yes, seals.

> **GM**

241

You know they even have cool milk here? It's very good. Mmmmmm, it's *sooo* good. It's made from dehydrated monkey babies... that they use in experiments. You know, cholera... it's considered a form of seasoning. They use it in smoothies.

                    RICK
But doesn't that bother you that they beat seals and dolphins?

                    GM
Oh, it's a horrible thing. You know they also do it to a very expensive breeds of poodle species' pungent feces? And kittens, too. Kittens are a delicacy in Eastern Romania. They hang them by their paws and beat them on the heads; and kittens are very resilient. It takes at least 12 strokes with an extremely blunt instrument.

                    RICK
That's horrible!

                    GM
Oh, it's horrid.

                    RICK
It's a travesty

                    GM
Oh, it's a complete travesty... and a tragedy as well. That would be a great board game: *Travesty and Tragedy*.

Another GLIB MAN in the booth adjacent pops his head over and addresses Glib Man.

                    GLIB MAN 2
Why don't they make board games anymore?

GM
In Sri Lanka they use board games for roofs

Glib Man as a Superhero

A robber is holding a gun up to a woman. Glib Man enters and sees this.

"Are you going to shoot her? Oh, you are completely going to shoot her...

"You know, in uhhh... South Afghanistan you would be considered a hero, or they would water board you and cut your ear off...

"I think they do that in other countries, too."

The robber becomes disgusted as Glib Man's reaction to the event and leaves.

This is the Excited Table

I'm sick of Rick Perry. I'm sick of people saying "that's how they are."

"That's how they are…"

He sounds like George Bush"

"It was my false promise of…"

It would all be ok if people would,"

No no, I ain't apologizin'. It's not just "raise your fuckin' blood," loser, Mary fuckin' Dipshit. Celery (in your drink). Your lifestyle. Fake palm tree-itus disease. We have this fuckin' goddamn malaise. You'd say, "Why, but he sounds like George Bush," or "He's another Bush, he'll cut jobs."

Cut jobs? Yeah that's good. Great. Cool. Fiery. Fierce. Yeah.

What men you use? What men?

"Cut jobs. Start with 35,000. Yeah, thirty-five thousand. It doesn't matter if the mail is slow for us."

Yeah, you get yours Fed Exed. Yeah, wait for mail, wait to eat but you guys, lemme get this straight, Bob, you men, what men, as I call, you, you eat immediately. You get to work your jobs immediately.

What jobs? Cut jobs. What men? Where are the men? What men? You cut jobs. What jobs? 35,000.

35,000 men. What men? Thirty-five thousand dollars. What dollars?

I don't see men. I don't see jobs. I don't see dollars.

"Wake up, men!"

No need to wake 'em up, they don't have to go to work, today. Today. Today. But you got your jobs, your dollars. What men.

We go and you lose your whole point of fuckin' view on your way to the glass being on its way to you... mmmmmm.... Ahhhh... sit back on tired fuckin' Sunday and tryin' hard to not think about coming Monday much less the reality of Rick Perry beyond the election.

Capturing why they're posturing. How could he posture, pander, and placate. You say "it's politics." No. Your politics. No. It's in *your* world. I say mine! *My* world! *My* politics! Your world ain't bloody Mary, ain't gonna change.

"No dude..."

It disappears. Be that guy. Be those guys. Be the army of... be the strong, massive march of "We all just wanna make it disappear." Cairo did. A woman did. A child did. But they both revealed how quick and strong they are... but this society, in your mind, wants us all to be weak... hold on, fucker, you fuckin' Bloody Mary life0styler, don't hear it and stupidly, robotly, agree and say, "I know I know they want us all to be weak." You think **YOU** wanna be weak?

Sip. "Oh, thank god I'm weak... mmmmmmm," *sip* "So I was drinking my Trendy Mary..."

Rick Perry you fucking giant garbage dump of a man. How would you like to be a walking garbage dump of a man?

"I'm Rick Perry. I'm Perry. I'm Bachman. I'm all of 'em. All of 'em. I'm all of 'em. I'm Obama. I'm the Rick Perry Obama-monster and I'm in a Navy Blue suit, a Navy Blue suit... ahhhh... I've done a LOT for Texas... I think society needs... *hahahahahaha*... I think society *needs*... Did I say society, I meant this *country*! There's no such thing as society. I'm the Rick Perry Monster. Corporations will save us. Corporations will save me. Us. You. You better listen to fucking me or... my daddy's gonna spank me."

Displaying Their Wares

Displaying their wares, their big glowering teeth, their oversleep eyes, exaggerated in their stupid walks, that display like dripping St. Bernard, walks. Great Danes, like Senators exaggerating the niceties of their humongous monster sweetness. The overused, misused, misallocated, misused funds and smiles. Their greedy dollar-spinning eyes and truth-praying need-crushing lies, false-promising lies, the "We try harder," cries, name-that-price gameshow, Pay the Price and eat Ramen Noodle and now just rice left over from your emptying the coffers and covert offer, steak-and-lobster walk, bouncing baby cow-killing future babies

Michelle Bachman

Hell-oh... Hell-oh pee-puhl.

My good, and uh, and that's the people we... we want and I know. We... Weeeee, as good pee-puhl, we... you and I... want... sss... sss... our coun-try... we... weeee... we... you and I... want our... our coun-try eee.... Eeeeee.... Eeeee... Baaaacckkkkkkkk... to where it once was, to where it can be. A great country. A powerful country. A mass-murdering country. With absolute freedom for those of us... we and... you and I... and us... we're big, large, uh... you and I... we business, yours, mine, our corporations uh... no reg-u...

We're tired of government busybodying themselves in our business big business good pulsating glowering like my face bloated like my face towering leaning over like me to thrive like my estates my yacht, to stay afloat.

I... with your help because it actually cannot thrive and fester and suck your money out of your life forces without your help because that's what each and absolutely every American is, a force to feed the monster of this great country.

I... we... you *and* I... us... them... those over there that you can *never* see, the three top money-earners and us can be giant hogs shoving the shit-filled pipeline into the giant humongous ass of an overgrown baby calf. An uncontrollable meat money-sucking monster.

And thank you, housewives.

Housewives, terrorize your husbands into two jobs

East Fuckin' Coast

"Where are you from? Are you from New York, bro,? East Coast?"

EAST MUTHER-FUGGIN' COAST. BROADWAY SHOWS, BEST RESTAURANTS IN TOWN, COFFEE, DONUTS, AND CIGARETTES... *You gotta problem? You gotta problem?...* SHOPPING, EATIN' CHOCOLATES, MARTINIS, AND RUNNIN' AROUND TOWN... *Nah, you were fuckin' lookin' at me...* DINERS AND STREETCORNERS, FASHION TOWN AND DISCOS... *You tell me one more time you weren't lookin' at me. You say that again. I'll knock you in the next fuckin' room, I'll knock you in the next fuckin', you were lookin' right at me...* WILD NIGHTS AND HAPPY DAYS, STROLLIN' THROUGH THE FUCKIN' PARK... *Hey! Miss! You need a nice guy? In your ass? My buddy, here, is a little lonely. CUNT! Why are you such freakin' bitches?...* COOL JOBS AND...*Drop this bag, Ricky. You fuck this up, you die, just drop the bag off, you fukkit-up, you die...* EAST MUTHER FRIGGIN' FUCKIN' COCK-SUCKIN'COAST.

Pockets

Funny thing. Amazing. I gotta tell ya what's blaring at me... blaring and glaring, doin' the blare-n-glare. D'ya know what "blaring" means? OK, jus' checkin'. Haahawahahah.

Well there was a few minutes, like the first second that immediately grabbed me, like slo-mo... the first sec, then slo-mo lookin' right at me. She's like water if it... she's BUTTER, she's *cream*, she's... her eyes glide, noticing, then landing into her She.

Up and down. Chin... lowers, then...

Oh, she is the whole, absolute... she is the woman, eternal girl whose lightning bolt is Then.

See. Look. Watch it: Then exhaltated. *Then* her eyes look a quick curve.

Her directness... woah.

Then she smiles to herself. Man, she can *do* that. She fuckin' does it.

Man... then I get mad, then frightened by her smile's way.

Hues... hues.

I would've trusted.

Her hair is daunting. It makes butter, water and mist peer and watch her hair: smooth, flowing. Man, it's like the night reveals what is made of... what the night truly is, what secrets and play are, what sultry, natural is. Sultry, natural, man. Sultry, natural.

Look, I bet... yeah, she's got back pockets! I imagine her slipping each hand, no, her *hands*... each hand... her hands... each... No, NO! Her *fingers*, her skin... her fingers as she slides, glides... as she slides, glides, slides... Slips! Yeah man, *that's* it, *she* slides as she slips her hand... her *hands*... slide.

Man, slide into her – each – pockets. Her each pockets. Her pockets.

Man get it. Get this. *Get this* you motherfuckers: Her teasing, inspiring fingers, each one slowly creates more and more continuous wonder. In my gut. Yours, too. Don't fuckin' lie to me.

I want to talk to her but I can't lie to her.

Everything out of her mouth was brilliant because of how her lips presented it and her eyes expressed it… expressed herself. But was it herself? Now I'm battling with nuances. Nuances skilled with footwork and speed. But with her no combos: just surprises, not practiced.

You ever force yourself to pay attention to something you'd ordinarily ignore? Like, "Oh my god, look how beautiful her fingers are."

Like there's… Remember when you were a kid, girls smelled like rubber? They had a weird smell? They were so cute they'd make your ears crackle?

Individual Men.

Individual men. 'Cause he was bouncing nimbly just off the floor.

Look up better word than "nimbly."

He was showing you and gods were slightly bragging like he was displaying... like he was a charm on their shining unreachable... shining brass ring... unattainable shiny object.

Like he was displaying cheap knives on a clean countertop but every time "Thelonius" or "Apartment" was said you saw him almost breakin' away from the law of "I Can't."

Aww c'mon man, don't be right, be free.

He couldn't do it. He didn't know there was a mountain there or more speed or more, uhh, dissatisfaction or more fuckin' pissedness at the way men are ripped off, never knowing the "True" of "No True": themselves versus The Other Guy, the other Himself.

How stupid, stupid is this setup, where a man can only feel the animal. No, I *want* to feel the animal but a man can only feel like a man when he plays pool or hits you with some lingo, some metaphor for "faggot," or weakness or fear or sensitivity.

Hey man, I've rarely... no... I've seen these guys, been with these guys, been these guys still am; and I've never *been*, I *am* this, that guy, *you*. I *am* you. *Those guys* are you. You only get to see them in a Ray Liotta or De Niro movie: it's called *Humanity*.

Sometimes it's broken leaders, guys who didn't know, weren't told but were built to lead or maybe, probably, no *definitely* to *not care*: to be too steady for your goals, too rich and fierce to try any walk through Halogen Hell – a purgatory of you sipping port with cheap cheese callin' it funny fuckin' phony names as all these men burn.

Nah, they don't ... They're trees... No, they're men, guys. So's me. So am I. So I will always love men and boys with eyes, men with big eyes and little moments, boys with slippery, slidin', smooth dignity.

The Homeless Guy [on a bench]

A homeless man is lying on a bench. The bench has a Real Estate ad on it featuring a female Real Estate agent. A man in a business suit walks up and asks him to move.

"I was married twice, why do you think I'm on this bench? All her cousins wore snowflake sweaters. She spent all my money on sheets. The rules, schools… Houseless, there's a difference. I'm houseless, not homeless. There's a difference.

"Nice bench. It's nice for no reason. You could try to create reason. An outside thought leads to Outside for me, because if I don't hold on to that bench then I gotta smell my piss in *your* life. And that's where Cake and Eat It Too Avenue exists. And then I gotta get stares from the ones who deem themselves the deemed followers of the deemed Deemed One, deemed Deemed by the deemed Deemed followers.

"You have heat, I need her picture for heat. You jack off a little bench music, the fantasy lives for me. She's the muse of the writhing, bold temptress in a pantsuit. Real Estate my ass, this girl here is the stuff bad movies are made of, and I mean BAD little girl.

"See, this is how serious what you own is. The life you build comes down to kickin' me off a bench. So you can, what, get two more dollars in that little business you got goin' on? It's shady here and I ain't bakin' for you little Bobby. I ain't Bakin', I ain't sittin', fryin', not even dyin'. I'm sayin' this prolonged torture, heat and stench prison camp now," he slaps the bench and hops on, "This here bench, this bench is where I can hear the prairie sluts at night and breezes whisper so faintly that you can only imagine the sweet meanness of their secrets.

"Now you feel right takin' that away from me? You wanna take my baby, Real Beauty Estate, from me? You have no idea the importance of my schedule. My hours are tricky in how they're lived. Whatever happened to real cowboys or any cowboy at all? You know what this bench means to me, this bench? Not *that* bench, stench alley over there.

"Wife? Oh man, my wife... Give me a woman with mud on her tits and asphalt on her butt. I'm serious about this woman, this being that constantly hovers. The woman on the sign, I'm serious about her, this being that constantly hovers, gazing at me. She...

"I book my own hours, I wander at 3AM, eat at 2AM. I read newspapers all night or just wander... roam. I roam or stare. I sit. I used to go to donut shops. Too many fringe people, it's like,'Man, have money or not.' Don't be talkin' crap about it. I ain't got no money.

"My first wife had me arrested. I had to hold my ex-wife down after she screamed and screamed and turned into Cape Fear. Her vagina turned into Cape Fear, a torrential, industrial gush. Her voice turned into ugly men's eyes.

"I don't like bosses. I don't like even bein' asked to leave this bench, this place from which my existence springs. This is where I gestate, alchemize, toss, turn, and face the torture of a man like me even though I'm a boy and a floating genius, see. I see you. You are the muse, enemy as muse. If only his poem I wrote about, here, like Picasso or Hunter Thompson staring at a girl on the beach. What did Hunter see? What did Picasso see? What would Henry Miller see?

"This is my Real Estate. You sell illusions. You know, I got fence, the family, a car, the estate, the rich guy. Now calls the perpetuation of floaters. The floaters float when their boats that are stirred quietly away from the waters of their own desperation. You're a picture. You become a picture. I give up this bench and you're a dead seal, a walkin', slidin', bus-ridin', car-drivin' ghost. Real Estate? You sell false states.

"I am a boy with a bench. I'm a boy with a bench, MAN with a bench. Man Bench."
The man in the suit offers the homeless some money.

"Money, oh yeah, that's the thing. A wife who sells real estate homes to homeowners, to homewivers."

Shy Boy

I'm the Shy Boy, I'm the one who fucks my life up. I'm the Why Boy, becomes a Tragic Boy, I drop things. I mess 'em up. I come to the home even though I told 'em all 'No More.' Them never touched. You burned me. I never forgot you wanted to kill me. I am the Shy Boy. My head is down, boy. My breathing hurts. My breathing hurt. I'm the dirt. I play in the dirt, all I ever did, dirty. I was a tiny thing, I was a thing. I was a thing. I am the Shy Boy, standing in the dark under the tree. The fucking tree. The dark. Why can't I be a Day Guy, an [unknown] and stick my head out, you know. But you ain't there. Stick my Day Guy head out of the door, the bright day, door, landscape, the archway, the bright, Day Guy archway. Not a Party Guy, truly want to be in the dark, under the tree, hands hanging, wide-pointed, focal-pointed vocal scream. I'm doin' it to me, I am worth nothing. Nothing has been the other sigh as I slide away from all that's given, no, worked for. I am the Dropper. I'm the Dropper, the Dropper, I drop things, things always being… Jumping down, I jump down, I pick it up. Like the orange juice story. I don't do things right, I am the Space Kid. It's what I had to do. I'm a Tenacious Boy. The Sparkle in Her Eyes Boy. Her eyes are wide, boy. Why he's got, why, why not me, boy? Hey God, wrong idea, I'm GOD, boy. Her eyes exist, boy. Do they live, boy? God, don't, boy. I'd Wild with her, boy. I'm a child, boy. I'm a Shy Boy, all kept inside, boy. My thoughts create and imagine, boy, scared to let 'em out, boy. Keep the lid down, boy. Push it out, boy. I'd rather stay inside, boy. I hate it inside, boy. Helen of Troy, toy, with the ideas, boy. Flirt, talkin' to yourself, myself, boy. I ain't scared, boy, to let it out, boy, I just don't know how, boy, ain't nohow, boy. I ain't no cow boy. I am the cowboy.

Mean Eyes

Some guy set up a financial arrangement for us to pay him means I'm waitin' to be seated by that phony reality-show, self-important, secretly self-hating, shaved head, pissy dick. He's gonna make me stand to be impressed by attitudes, airs, and some brand name.

Fuck, man, even the pope's sleazy these days. I just need to cross the border, man, and even if I did, I'm hungry and I deserve food. It's my bein'-born given right. [because he won't wait to be seated]

And he sits down. And the guy looks at him, scrutinizing like he didn't wait all night.

"Yeah, coffee brother. Thanks a lot. Mean Eyes!"

And the waiter goes, "Excuse me?"

"I'm seein' mean eyes, man, easy. You heard me. And did you hear 'asshole' come outta my mouth? The answer is, 'no.' No. So leave it at that. Mean, intense, driven eyes but you gave up. We all do from time to time. Hey man, I'm just tryin' to connect. I'm Woolworth's, Best Buy and I'm only trying to sell you me.

"Mean eyes, possible no-shit kinda guy, I like that. The world does too only you were never told that and you know what, you should be told. I ain't finished, yet and I ain't no sound bite [because the other guy comes over] and if you wait you might be moved by a passer-by. IF YOU WAIT YOU MIGHT BE MOVED BY A PASSER-BY, someone who is now in your life... NOW. So, OK, I'll give you some [unknown] leeway. You got smart eyes, run with it. Run with it! Coffee good here, brother?"

"Sir, is there a problem?"

"Oh, man, forget this place."

Citizens' Access

There's this joke about the citizens not having access to their so-called political leaders.

Why'd the citizen shoot that lady?
    Because he wanted to kill Sarah Palin and didn't have access.

Why'd the guy rob the bank?
    He knew who was robbing him, but he didn't have access to their board room.

Why'd the citizen choke that old man?
    He wanted to choke his senator, but he didn't have access.

Big Time

How did Hitler escape under the radar for so long, how'd he go unnoticed for so long?
Anybody who says "Big time," you don't take them seriously.

Do you think Hitler ever used the expression, "Big time?"

> "I'm going to murder six million Jews, big time!"
> "Alright, okay, Hitler. Sure you will."
> "Jews are evil, big time!"
> "Well, not all of 'em, Hitler."
> "No... big time!"

This Just In

Michelle Bachman admits she's ugly on the inside and that she's a liar. Rick Perry jumps on the national conversation bandwagon and admits the leak was true: the private conversation that revealed that he sees himself as the ugly man he's been since age 6.

From his 6th birthday on, he was forcibly sent to take dance class with the world famous Bush Dance Clan. He spent years in the Clan Class learning the art of shifting his feet and shrugging his shoulders and was eventually groomed to enter the real world by exchanging his tutu for a blue suit tutu and he became a Shifty Shifterfoot, advanced to foot shrugging and mugging eyes, glowering so wild his nickname in the political community, his moniker, became Dances with Glowering Smiles.

He and Michelle Bachman eventually, at the age of 8, were voluntarily forced by their parents to enter the master class of Condeleeza Rice where the Master Glower defeats society, where the powerful ancient art of Glowering Scumbag masks dancing ass-kiss prancing. Bought and paid for, make-you-sick-of-America glance class with no class, just dance-with-your-ass class to win the fake face in your face race.

Tonight at 10, Sarah Palin wants you to suck her tits, well, let's do that now. Sarah Palin, in the studio now, wants poverty-stricken, foreclosed Americans to, quote, "I just want every dumbed-down, warped, disposable American or trampled, down-trodden, used up by our blessed, heaven-sent, deemed-by-Jesus, show-me-the-money, bling bling, bang bang, and, who could ever forget, BOOM BOOM CHRIST ALMIGHTY to know that when times get rougher, and they will get rougher, well they can suck my tits anytime, day or night, 24/7/11. They can suck my big nasty momma-lucious breasts at any time. I'll be your dog and you can ride this pony, because I'm a mother and a leader and I'm here for you. You can always find me smoking against the mirror at the Dog-and-Ponies Smoke-and-Mirrors theme park."

Jobs Now

Your wife has a job, if she chooses to show up or get back into the real-estate or fucking fundraising business. Your daughter has a job when she's not travelling or talking about the tall Euro-cunt she met in Europe. Your son has a job, after golf and crew and swiming in the hot springs and blue seas of your resort hotel: pot-head, coke-head. Your maid has a job, her husband has a job, her kids have jobs, your neighbors have jobs, your plumber has little odd jobs — all these in your company. Jobs Now.

They have "Jobs Now." You created "Jobs Now." But creating jobs? Fuck you, "Creating Jobs" that you have now. Give us those, these, that you have now, could create now. Now.

Invest in citizens. Citizens? People.

Working man — people.

Invest. Not in the country. The country? Invest in women, invest in men, invest in that girl, invest in those girls, invest in that boy, the boy, those boys, those women, those men. Those. These boys, these girls, these little girls, these teenage girls, these grown-ups standing over here. Discussing you, rolling their eyes.

He, rolling his eyes.

He, rubbing his worried neck.

She, not knowing what is done now.

By you.

What is?

Now.

Secretly done.

By you.

Now.

Now.

And now.

Now.

And now again.

Immediately.

But we must be too desperate. We can't seem too desperate, come off too desperate, appear too desperate.

You got jets 'cause you're desperate.

Urgent and Need.

Must have Results.

These kids, these boys, these girls, these guys. Guys and ladies. Be a guy instead of what you are being. Where you must die.

Jobs.

Now.

Or.

Die.

Now.

You create job-creating plans. Jobs Now. You create death, now: her, him, that little girl, dies. That little boy. He will find you and create what you've created.

Take your kids' wi-fi and high-tech giant flat-screen... instead of buying 'em shit, open businesses here. They give their mistresses jobs, yachts, trips, diamonds... Diamonds... Diamonds

DI... A... MONDSSSS.

And they, these fake lovers fake laugh at these real liars.

Bad jokes for top dollar at high-end low-life benefits. These mistresses, these candidates, bend over and lift their skirts. The corporations shouldn't be giving a shit.

The money you give the girlfriend you left your so-called wife for, that money in gifts should be the new 99 Cent store with more employees. And any stupid, politically savvy, asinine, so-called tough, defensive, right-wing, hand-me-down thinker, machine rationalizer must be told, "You don't care about people, so shut up."

So yeah, I'm a Softee. It's time for Softees: people who can't stand abused dogs, cats, kids, and other strays in any realm. People are vegans, vegetarians, and non-labeled labeled ones: Softees, as faggot Republicans say. Softees must get hard now.
It's time for hard cock and wet pussy to be the new running mates 'cause the suits, the "true blues", the truth-hindin', money-slidin', avalanche creatin' everywhere, it's time for them to shut up.

If all we care about is money, they won.

These mistress-fuckers with their disgusting eyes and bodies. These are the true old men. "Well, you gotta this and that," No, You gotta! You do! Stop sayin' what "we" gotta understand and do something. DO.

Not "down-the-line", not "we're hoping so", not "it should pay off", not even "it will pay off". Stop saying, "Eventually," or "we'll," or "first we gotta," or "down the line," or the worst, "ten years from now per projection." Stop saying that or I'll find you, tear your wife's ring off, open a business with it and hire 100 more workers.

And stop smilin' about what you foresee while he/she/they/me die and die and die, and you still look at your fuckin' loser liar pig mistress. Stop workin' harder than those who got jobs to create the lie that Wall Street is. For us.

You hider. You are a monstrosity. You create monstrosities causing, making, building out of our bones, atrocities. Your atrocities.

Hey, how does it feel to be an atrocity, you fucking pinstripe? You pinstriper of pinstripers. You don't impress me, you *depress* me.

Hey, there are seething liars hiding in the house, eating our food. Monkeys actually have more life and are more intelligent than you. Rick Perry, Michelle Bachman, Mitt Romney, and Sarah Palin, even Hillary Clinton. The fact that we have to wait for jobs to be created. The fact that jobs were lost, homes were lost for no reason other than More Profit.

No reason other than MORE PROFIT.

No reason other than MORE PROFIT.

These depress people, the people that have been depressed by this warhawkian, war-based, every-excuse-under-the-sun based economy of a country. But they've been trying to smother us minute-by-minute.

I mean, Michelle Bachman's been saying these hurricanes and floods and earthquakes are God trying to get our attention, that we need Republicans back in office. No, God's too smart for that. If anything... if ANYthing...

If he says ANYthing, he says, "Politicians are the same as tornados, are the same as hurricanes and the flood mowing over you and me." See, God digs myths and metaphors: look at Adam and Eve.

And if you have a liar in your house you get depressed. And if you have somebody who cops to what he's been doing, who says, "I gotta give, I gotta help, I mean look at all I got," in the middle of the street, "this ain't charity, this is just 'cause it feels right. We're alive. I have way too much. Here, let me invest or just start you up or you can share my knowledge or muscle."

HORROR

I will tell you the horror:

- Your old man with his hand crashing down on you. CRASH CRASH CRASH!
- Pissing your pants daily at school.
- Being a child athlete and having your parents beat it out of you, then offering you cake.

The REAL horror is judging yourself, that's the real horror; judging yourself for every action you take:

- Yesterday's horrors of sucking dick.
- Heroin and social security offices.
- Homelessness.
- Where do I sleep?
- Incest.
- My father beating me.
- Where do I eat?
- My brother's face on my body.
- Having money, making money, then having it all stolen, borrowed, spent, and lost.
- Ex-girlfriends.
- Ex-friends, friends that aren't real... Liars.
- Being a vegan.
- The color *Mango*
- Waking up after a twenty-year career with 4 and 5-star reviews from a car accident that removed my memory and left me to rebuild my mind, my hands, and my ability to keep my pants from dropping to the floor.
- Not being able to use a fork, a pen, or know my best friend's name. *Horror*

ALL horrors, but I dealt with them. I survived, to a point, all of this.
But the real horror, the REAL HORROR, is what I'm dealing with today:

- Self doubt.
- Girls that use the term "awkward".
- Dating
- The word "obscene". I am not obscene.

- Judgment on my material by me, by others, by an industry or community that refuses variance.
- Indifference.
- Love... a COMPLETE horror.

Today's horrors outweigh any of the self-induced worries of yesterday because today's horrors I cannot control:
- The uneducated
- The illiterate
- Those that refuse to read, but can
- The GAP
- American Apparel
- Burger King
- Our government
- The war(s)
- Our nation
- Religion
- Things that impact me, which I'm powerless to change

DOOMED TO NEVER MAKE IT

Doomed to never make it
He's always gotta fake it.

We're awaiting word on two projects.
They're showing a lot of interest.
Things are great, things are great!

We're waiting on their calls
Should happen before the fall.
Next fall… no NEXT fall
NO, not THAT fall
"The one that's farthest away?" he asked
They said, "It's not that far,
In twenty years you'll have a car."
And the chorus sings: "Just think of that!"

He's seen so many fakers,
The bottom-feeding takers
Talking 'bout the Lakers
"Hey," *high five* "Hey," *high five* "Don't leave me hangin', bro"
"Yeah, cut the rope, put him down here,
"Oh damn, it's Rick Shapiro."

And the other guy says something worse than, "Who?":
        "Oh yeah, I heard of him,
        "I heard once he got angry,
        "I really liked what he did
        "But I never admitted it or said it out loud,
        "'Cause I'm an American
        "And that's how we crawl
        "And hide dark against the wall."

Suzanne

Suzanne, man. MAN! Fuck this. You the greatest. You are. I ain't drunk. Don't commiserate. I got wide faith in weird results 'cause this is a blip.

God, I HATE this, tellin' me 'bout their fuckin' PIANO skills 'n there's this Australian future volleyball champion… This tall lil' girl who's gonna pick 'n not fall. The victorious explosion of choosing the act of choosing.

Mice in the apartment with their feet up. AHHHHHH, choosing, wouldn't that be a nice toe in the moment.

Cockroach to trust yourself to be in the…

Shrink chooses to be in the moment… I'm going now to be in the moment.
> *Oh no, here comes the guilt and fear.*

The Shrink, he worries about… he is afraid. He is afraid of what people think:
> Ricky, in fact I'm not afraid of what people think. I'm just a living infant. Then I see their angry eyes, frightened by an idea of what and who I might be: a seer, a truth wanter.

RICK

Yeah, you could see her little, cool, luscious shoulders, her lil' tits as she bent over to reach for something in front of you, wishing and deeply wanting a parallel universe where it's all ok and it's all experienced. All your desires exist, and the having... you have to look at the problems in society. I get it now. I get it. Then we delete their friend requests and get our sons and daughters to Twitter it or some shit, 'cause eye-to-eye don't matter no more.

There's a human being here, this fucking child molester-eyed little frightened tiny teeny-eyed prick shrimp-dick. This kayaking diaper man: he can't look me in the eye, but he can email my manager one word or else it was my back hurting: the STRESS! Fuckin' lost my mind in LA, fuckin' LOST MY MIND!

Lost my hands, I wanted to hit so many people so many times, these fucking bloody little snits.. who walks around like this? Who walks around like this, these dickless strollers, Twitter 'n Facebook 'n pretty colors, but who's touchin'? Who's grabbin'?

Yeah, we're faster now. Our 'Now' is faster, but the immediacy, the urgency to see another person... I'm going home to sleep.. but before was pot 'n coke... now.. *Stayin' home...*

Then it was the internet and then it was reality TV, now it's Facebook givin' the desired result. That result; not your homework, your IBM management results, but human.

Ohhh so human taste buds placed on your taste buds and she is writhing, giving and fucking and making out and she keeps coming to your door asking for more. "Hi, can I want some more?"

Then I notice her feet in some poetic way, some half-way. This crummy life where you gotta cut back to... hmmm... interesting...

Fuckin' interesting. Hmm...

They get along like little puppies, I mean they're so wonder-fucking-ful. Who cares? I'm a human baby. It was a fucking hooker I went to and didn't know. It was ok. I didn't know I could have had the girl over there. I died 'n went to AA, then decided – GODDAMMIT, WHERE'S MINE?!?

Where's my girl?

IN BED

Last night I was sitting up in bed, the corner of my queen-sized bed wanting bad crummy things. Like wanting to fuck. Fantasizing about fuckin' my niece, and my other niece, too.

"Awwwwwwww"

DON'T 'AWWW' ME. Don't Church-Mule this stuff!!! A man's look… listen, I'm tryin' to talk… to discuss! Why don't you wait and hear the humanity knockin' on your ears, man!

"Yeah, but you don't gotta tell people this kind of stuff?"

SEE! SEE!!! THAT'S where you make yourself a piece of garbage. Did you hear me? Were you wasting and fucking up my life and time by saying that I tell people this??? MAN, where are the listeners? That's why advice sucks… falls short, no, becomes the very thing that ruins life. I'm telling you something and you, "awwww" like your acquired listening skills just deflect…

"Well ok… but I… well… ok."

I'm thinking about fuckin' my niece. I'm thinkin if I'm gonna die, then I'm gonna be over, man, like I never existed and I don't care or can't experience their remembrance of me. They think about you one second, then they're into their search for happiness and it's just a thought… gone away!

So I want to go into a dark, shitty, but exciting life: coke, smack, men's wives I don't know. Then, you're dead! I mean, I don't, do NOT at all want to have… no… I wasn't born with an affinity for the richness in life. I'm lost… gone… deep down, I know it.

"Deeper down. What's there? I'm asking for the truth from you. I got it… so… deeper down."

Well, not moralistically. I'm not gonna answer you with a moralistic acceptance of what's supposed to be there.

"Oh."

Deeper down... maybe a warmth, a desire for expansion and growth like you're sitting with relatives and they discuss their fuckin' kids... Yeah, I want that, but then these ugly promises of youth extended, defiance enjoyed with ugly, appreciative baby dolls.

"That's your illusion."

I hug the man's wife and stroke her back.

HELP

Then I gotta keep my eye on people that believe the bullshit. They made themselves out to be rash

I mean just waiting for someone to fix and cure their ailing situations. Animals, no, worms…

I've done that
I've tried that
I've been fucked by that

I hate that word now. I don't want to help them. I mean, I'm going to be dead in…

REAL

She gave me this uncanny Real. "Girl" Real. What a blowjob is about: hunger, no, freedom, no, just what a mouth, head, and body is for.

Rick Shapiro on Closing Gitmo

They just found out that Obama's terrorism tactics are like Bush and Cheney's. Obama's applauded them in his speech recently and he told the progressive that he wouldn't resort to this same thing. It's like when he said Gitmo was closed, and then it's open and then it's closed.

Obama's the new Bush.
"Gitmo's closed, I promise. The healthcare bill needs more adjustments."
So does my dying mother.
Gitmo, open again. Closed. Open. Closed. Almost. Not yet. Closed. Definitely.
"I know. OK, pass the health bill but don't tell anyone."
I hear it in my ears: rise patriotically Japan, America, Japan, America. Where's the flag, Japan? Where's the flag, Japan? Where's the flag, Japan?
Stars and Stripes now! Salute! Stars and Stripes, pow pow! Japan. Toyota. Destruction.

I said that just because [Obama] promised in [the 2008] election that Guantanimo would be closed. As if it really mattered to us.

"But I promise, that'll be my first thing."
Dammit, it **doesn't** MATTER, I don't care what anybody says. It doesn't matter to us, "My father loses his home but you promise to close Gitmo."
Fuck you.
Ya know? Save that for the human rights organizations, great. That's just too black and white, man.

It's good to hear Japan's back in the news, it makes me feel American

Amorous Inner Rumblings

When am I gonna feel, go out and get love? Listen. Boom boom boom boom. You hear the drums, the poundings and poundings? Amorous inner rumblings?

Amorous inner rumblings, does that mean nothing to no one?

Amorous inner rumblings.

Amorous inner rumblings.

Not the little bells of *like*. Amorous inner rumblings like Indians or angry starving revolutionaries or a room full of your angry fucking psychotic old man.

COWBOY

Hey, kid, do you like guns? It's gorgeous, the sounds o' bullets. The moment they're released from their chambers. See that's like you, the ugly/beautiful chambermaid, the beauteous chambermaid bein' released from her chamber.

See? We're all bullets. All us bullets, deep down, sleep. But they lie in wait. We lie in wait.

Wait! Maybe they sleep until they're fired! By the Firer. By the situation.

The Firer is in the whole setup!

My true poetic nature? This *is* my true poetic capture! If she's a hooker, I'm lucky.

No I'm not.

Or maybe she'll be a lizard. The embodiment of my infinite nature. If she crawls, I want her. If she walks, she's too efficient. That arrogance.

Maybe it's a fucking guy who comes out of the shower with donuts.

Stroller

Don't you ever see those ladies with the thousand-dollar strollers? Don't you hate them especially when your girlfriend looks over at you or up at you if she's short or down at you because she's tall or just condescendingly at you 'cause that's her way? She looks at you, without saying a word, "When us? When us? When us?" And you tell her, "I would have a kid except I hate 'em."

"Oh really? I just…"

"I don't want a GAP baby with that stupid hat. If ever I have a kid, I want it to be a Born-to-Ride baby, a biker at age 1, MC jacket, with their muddy fruit-of-the-looms with half a nut hangin' out and cowboy boots, the ones I'm savin' for him or her. The ones I had at age 1…"

Are you kiddin'? He shot out o' the womb wearin' 'em!

"OK? Get it? Life is unfair and it sucks sometimes. Suck my fucking dick. I don't have time for the worries. They can commiserate by the potato salad at the reunion with all the aunts and uncles."

The Meaning of Life

When asked Rick about the Meaning of Life
I've never known this stance. It sounds like a stance more than a question. Hmmm, the meaning of life.

The meaning of life or, if you're a dull, mainstream dullard, here is the meaning of life... I ran away from an angry god. First I stood still, I mean I froze up and was taught only to never have a mind. I was taught **ONLY** to **NEVER** have a mind of my own.

"Now, for me..."

PERVERSE

You can sit with criminals and you can get perverse with a girl, for lack of a better word...

Language is so stuck, in my head, in this country.

Like if you use *perverted* you see three old women crossing arms, you see that in a flash. So you go, like, "**I** don't mean it the way **they** mean it," and so you struggle with some other word instead of the same *perverse*.

You know, it's not that you can get mean... but not mean, you can *play*. That's what I think is probably wrong, why you ask these questions, people have their own playfulness that they haven't been able to use out in the world.

Except for Tony Hawk and Harvey Keitel... and James Joyce.

Exciting Nature

She gets angry on a dime baby, she was a pig in hounds-tooth clothing. Her lying, uncaring, zombie-rolling-her-eyes-immediately-saying-and-doing-nothing; rolling her eyes at tall, bent, warped wood, small town, coward, chicken-shit. She was the chicken-shit. *She* was the chicken-shit, not me. *He* was the coward. He worked and worked and she worried and worried as they got annoyed at my explorative, exciting nature.

My exciting nature, my imagination, to shut me down; he/she/they wanted me out, dead. Deep within, hiding in their horse-shit. Their horse-shit... he used to say, "Ah horseshit!" and I would get struck down but the strong, smart part of me wondered, "Why horse-shit? Why horse-shit?" And now I ask, "Why did I think he was always right," even though he was completely stupid and utterly, utterly, damaging – destroying – me.

He was what wrong *is* and she was worse, her caring. She was so mentally ill. They were. I know it. I know it.

And they were status seekers. All status seekers are scared of life. Worse.

They: Babies that face that two-faced, eye-rolling, making them all feel the same way about me.

She: her skirts, her girdle, her hallway, her coffee, her ignoring, the ignoring, *only* ignoring me. Her violence to, at me: to me striking, pulling, screaming in the dark – stab-ass, stabbing, frightening me but I wasn't frightened of her.

And that's what they couldn't stomach.

Her stomach aches. "It's like a punch in the stomach." She chose him. I didn't. He chose her, I didn't. She chose to be a liar. Every lie. And to stay sickly, dying, cowardly lyin' violently, and hiding it in her girdle of hounds tooth shithead shit. Her stench. Her writhing, lying, fierce, no-deeming just demon, violent and lying, not fierce. She couldn't stop me as I left that place forever.

Families Dressing Families

Seem to have bought us the right clothes for each stupid sort of them, I mean, any of these, I mean, uh, citizens… I'm turning into a Republican. Take the words *Single Party System* out of the English-speaking, uh, vernacular. Replace those words with, uh, bipartisan and Domino's, KFC, new chicken, now has new wings. Wings wings new now NOW and NOW and NOW AND NOW FIESTA!

Isn't it fun to have an anxiety attack and look out your window, behind the curtain like in the commercials? Stun 'em with the side effects listing. Describe those side effects. Rapid. Recite it, the siiiiiide effects list…

- Tiger Woods' balls!,
- Nausea
- TMZ
- Blurred vision
- new NOW CELEBRITY

SNOW?

SARAH PALIN
When I found out Alaska had snow, I knew something had to be done about it.

RICK PERRY
Big eyes, deep donkey smile into macho mule chest push. Chest push, look left. Chest push, look right. Chest push and jaw-jut. Dumb-ass jaw jut. And lie and lie and lie. Stare into space. Leave the room out of fear but keep your empty burning body at the podium or table or wherever they didn't tell you were or weren't listening when they said, "Stay in your body, Rick Perry.

"Wait, what am I thinking? Leave whenever you want. In fact, just leave your teeth and your suit, we'll do the rest. Thank you."

They now do the jaw-jut chest pump. "Oh, we got your suit rigged for that. Each of your suits is rigged and your face pumps and jaw slides in your locker"

Rick Shapiro LIVE

... [Rick Perry] became a shifty shifter of feet, shrugging and mugging eyes glowering so well, his moniker became Dances with Glowering Smiles. He and Michelle Bachman at the age of 8, voluntarily forced by their parents, entered the master class of Condeleezza Rice where the Master Glower defeats society. And they studied in the class of the way more powerful ancient art of Glowering Scumbags Dancing Ass-Kiss Prancing Go Out And Pay For It Make You Sick of America Glance Class with no class, just dance-with-your-ass class, to win the face in your face race.

[APPLAUSE]

Nah, don't clap... all I really want to do is talk about how beautiful things are. Like the colors in that painting with the butterfly/dragonfly hybrid synergy with the fish [UNKNOWN] down with the fake desert and pretend redwoods [VOICE COVERED BY CAPPUCINO MACHINE]...

A beautiful statue holder without a statue that says, "Any human being if you need a statue that [you] should be remembered by," a table where there's no pretentious people. It's beautiful, man, there's nothin' like it. Look at that table with people acting pretentious, like, "It's just like when we were in Europe."

I hate being pretentious. It reminds me of when I read Nietzsche.

I woke up this morning and I weighed the world... wait, I should explain that. The first time I realized... you weigh the world. It's not that I'm sitting in the back of the café, judgmental, I'm weighing the world.

[INTERRUPTED]

One of the tables moved back... in my mind... but in reality... it's fine.

[INDIVIDUAL PASSES BY AND DUCKS]

Why're you... don't duck and cover, duck and roll.

Wait... here's the good part of the bit.

This just in... *Sarah Palin* wants poverty-stricken foreclosed Americans to "I just want every worked, disposable, dumbed-down American, our trampled, down-trodden, used by our blessed, heaven-sent, Jesus 'Show-me-the-Money Bling Bling Bang Bang and, who could ever forget, Boom Boom' Christ Almighty. I want people to know that when times get rougher, oh and they will get rougher, that they can suck my tits any time, day or night. 24/7-11. You can suck my big, nasty, momma-lucious breasts at any time. I'll [UNKNOWN] your dog and you can ride this pony to the show 'cause I'm a mother and a leader and I'm here for YOU. You can always find me smoking against the mirror at the theme park..."

I didn't finish that.

It was Hitler who said, "I will hurt humankind. And here's how I'll do it. I'll squint before I start the day."

That's my impression of a racist before he becomes a racist, he goes...

[RICK SQUINTS]

And then the thoughts come! The barrage of *nigger* and *heeb* and *faggot* and *pussy,* nonstop. Meanwhile he's just lookin' at you—THAT'S THE RACIST SQUINT

Let's Get 'Im

I played a caller on my radio show – pretended to be a caller. I said, "What's the meaning of life?"

I cannot believe there's a meaning of life when we all just are worm-food in the end, I mean, I keep my head down, I ruminate, I try to make sense of the beatings: the guys jumping out of cars. That's funny, I was thinking, guys jumping out of cars.

Isolate the incident: "There's one now!" All of a sudden these guys jump out. It's insane.

"Hey, there's an Iraqi, Black, Russian, Jew, Tranny walking. Open the doors. Let's get 'em!"

The worst expression ever invented by the devil was, "Let's get 'em."

You could say "Lock and Load" but it's really "Let's get 'em"

"Let's get 'em, the Heeb/Nigger/Puerto Rican/Faggot! Let's get 'em!"

...AND TAKE 'EM TO A MOVIE...

Another Attack of the Normals

I was in this café, usually crowded but on this day it wasn't. A woman goes up to this big jock – he was sitting on a counter looking out of a window with his computer and coffee – from her table on the inside. She walks up to him and I heard her whisper, "Excuse me. Could you... could you just watch my stuff? I have to go to the bathroom. It'll just... it'll just take a second... just a second."

I thought to myself, "What's weird about that?"

I looked around and we were the only three in there. She thought I was gonna steal her purse.

"Could you look after my laptop for just a minute," and I was the only other one there... in the place.

Normals. Brushing their teeth. You put on your jackets. Swing 'em on and then judge the jacket swing and judge and judge. Well I'm judgin' you. Like a rapist.

If you're not cool with me, I'm fuckin' up that Normal pussy you, normal pussy.

Toothpaste. You guys dig your toothpaste [UNKNOWN]. Man. Big rebel snake talking or a coyote.

And you dig brushin' *everything*. You brush your jackets. You brush your stupid bland normal, formal but informal sweater.
Normal, formal but informal: you look like you feel alright with your hide-and-seekiness.
Seek the deodorant. Seek the cock/stock/lock/porterhouse/ fiesta – you know – *casual* hair.

Too Good for His Job

You ever see someone who doesn't want to do his job? We all have those days, months and constant seconds.

"But don't take it out on me, I ain't your stupid Polish Ugandan manager. I just walked in. I did only that. I just... look... look, I went from *here* to *here*."

Or worse, you ever see the guy who thinks he's too good for his job? No, too good for any interaction with *you*.

I went to get a cup of coffee, that's all. Nothin' for the other guy to turn into a tiny, out-of-control, mini Wolverine Poodle.

I moved into a nice neighborhood, because I made a little bit of money from a TV show that I know is canceled now, because I'm back to jerkin' off behind boiler rooms and over there and over there and... over there. So I made a little money... well actually, that's not why I moved in to the nice neighborhood. The real reason I moved in was: you ever look into a girl's vagina and see beyond the vagina into the whole apartment and notice a brand new Hewlett Packard printer, an extra iPad, a high-def, 3d, flat-screen, and $30 she keeps in the dresser drawer where, if you push hard while fuckin' her, you reach in and take $10 out. If she catches you, push harder, her eyes roll into the back of her head, you take the $10, put it in your back pocket.

Always leave your jeans on during sex.

See, you learn somethin' at my shows.

So I went to a coffee shop in the neighborhood and it was all male-model wannabees workin' there. And the one who I was about to order coffee from was a tall male model but he had a bald spot so he's angry that he's not gonna be rich or good lookin' or neither or both. So angry – he's an angry male model. He's angry. He's got opinions but no thoughts.

So I ask for a cup of coffee from this guy and he puts milk in it and I say, "No thanks, I want it black. I'm a cop. I write pot-boilers naked with beer on my tits under a giant Bukowski poster as mice and roaches dance in a circle around my feet singing in unison that I'm a loser in all my ex-girlfriends' voices and glare at me, catching their breath, climbing up my chest, screaming in my ears in French and some Israeli religious epithets that I am a loser in more French."

He couldn't understand that but it felt better than sharin' it in AA. So I said, "I want it black."

And he did sort of a pseudo-sort-of-defiant-sort-of-stance, looking down at me like existence was taught to him to be not allowed to have someone like me in his life. And yet his need for me was all he had left in order to use his nauseating capacity to hand you dirty instances of condescension. He partnered it with a smug, "Tsk, tsk," and punctuated his response to my order with another, "Pft." And he seemingly victoriously, looked like an idiot, and he said, "…

The Beauteous Couple

"I'm just tryin' to make a friend. Aww, c'mon, man..."

> Like this is how I really want to be when I see a guy and a girl, where the girl's gorgeous, I guess. 'Cause I'm in L.A, now.

> OK, so the girl's gorgeous... and the guy's an ugly pig. I mean ugly like he fell down a flight 'a steps and he ain't stopped since.

A guy hits on the girl, "*blah blah blah blah... something poetic... blah blah blah blah.*"

"I'm just tryin' to make a friend. Aww, c'mon, man... I'm just tryin' ta... wait... you two a couple?

"You his girl?

"That's nice. That's the way it outta be, people outta be in love. That's right. It's your born, given right. I'm just tryin' to make a friend, c'mon, man. I'm just tryin' to make your eyes look in my eyes. C'mon, man. One honest word, Wordsworthless. C'mon. I know you believe in yourself. I know you got it goin' on. You're big in the game, Game Boy. C'mon, buddy, walk it like you talk it: long, tall, cool.

"This your lady? Man if you was my angel, baby, I'd tear you up. You'd be smilin' like... Aww, c'mon, man. I know you two gotta good thing. No one ever said... I didn't say you wasn't a beauteous couple with all the happiness you both deserve, I'm just tryin' to meet people in this town. I'm just tryin' to meet people I can trust.

"You know, baby. You know. Yeah. Still ain't met the real man you so long for. I KNOW, man. I know you're the deal, Dealio. I'm just sayin'... Aww, I'm sayin' somethin' wrong? Yeah, what is right? You tell me, motherfucker. You tell me bein' alone all night long... yeah, if there is a God he wants me to be the cool loner... the... the....

"You're the tight-ass slitherin' representation... no... EMBODIMENT of ALLLLL mankind's relief. Man you are the excited, unrequited symbol of dessert. You're the real, lickable cupcake, man. If you ain't unheard thunder, I don't know what is. Unheard thunder resounds inside you, never screaming your own sex-truth and erotic desires. You got dissatisfaction in the form of an agitated lonely panther. Ahhh… Ahhh….

"LEMME FINISH, MAN! Seventeen poems, two-hundred paintings, and a bottle of wild pills all in your lonely physicality. Alone. You lonely little passion hawk… DESCEND… WRITHE in cool king's flight. Downward, baby. Meet me on the insides of what the darkness reveals.

"I'm screamin' the end of your unfinished thoughts and continuous discovery of new explosions. You, your unsaid, startling eye flashes, your eyelashes… wild bobcat…

"Aww SCREW YOU, man! Like I can't have no women friends?!? I mean, what the hell is it with the people around here in this town? You all drink silent coffees and drown unknowingly in your pleasantries. Aww, c'mon, man… I'm just tryin' to make conversation, ain't that what you say, smalltalkers? God damnit! GOD DAMMIT!!!"

The man walks away. He sings, "I'm so ti-red 'a bein' alone, I'm so ti-red 'a bein' alone….

"Blue moon… you saw me standing alone…."

Sivananda

I went to a Sivananda Dancey Nancier class. No. I went to a Sivananda Dancey Nancier guru, to her center: Owned, Not Owned, For it Can Never be, Never Owned, Now in This Moment it is Yours Inc. I climbed a mountain then another in my neon DayGlo lavender jasmine-scented burlap spiritual Speedo full-length mountain-climbing goat scarf dressing of the male goddess.

Took a helicopter, hers, and climbed two more steps in my Buddha goddess demon animal fluffy devil opposing wandering sandals, into her penthouse shrine-esque...
> *Oh! Can you tell this is a search? Like you went to... Mecca?*

... and she told me, now remember, this woman is 129 years old and still prays before each post-tennis rum tofutti. She's never left the poverty-stricken surroundings, never been anywhere except Sri Lanka, Serengeti. Knows nothing...
> *I hate this...*

... Two steps in my Buddha...
> *...this got stuck... it's stuck [speaking about the computer]*

... So I climbed a mountain, then another one in my neon DayGlo lavender jasmine-scented burlap spiritual Speedo full-length mountain-climbing goat scarf dressing of the male goddess nutless hipster uniform, took a helicopter, hers, and climbed two more steps in my Buddha goddess demon animal fluffy devil opposing wandering sandals, into her penthouse shrine-esque and she told me – now remember, this woman is 129 years old and still prays before each post-tennis rum Tofutti...
> *I might change "tennis" with...*

... and prays after – she's never left the poverty-stricken surroundings. Never been anywhere but Sri Lanka, Serengeti. Knows nothing of outer other cultures, as she calls them, and remains in India to this day, moment, now, on, and when I told her I wanted to die, this 129 year-old woman offered me all she had left of her hand sanitizer and when I told her, "Fuck the world, I don't want it anymore," she told me this, the simplest, most obvious seeming, sizzling bacon piece of new truth, greater truth. She stared, and her stare, this is true, caused this burning sensation, and she touched my each eye and said, told me: *(in a Jewish mother voice)* "Sweetheart, you're too tense, try to relax, you know. Do you live near a pool or a park, even a grocery store? These things help me. My husband's very…

You know what, buy a nice new suit, you know? Because there are *so* many sales right now. Buying a suit don't help me, although I love pantsuits. I'll go put one on and you know what? I'm thinking you're not too different from my husband's size. Now come," she claps, "we'll put our suits on and go to my screening room or we can walk to the video arcade, they even have bumper cars. I can't go on them but I'll wave to you as you ride by. And take some of my special incense, you can give it to your family from me, a souvenir. "

COME BACK

I don't need her. I don't need her. Do you get it? Do you fuckin' get it? I'm glad she's gone. Rapturously glad. She was screamin' at my heart like an opera singer doin' the national anthem as it piquantly lowered into hell, yellin' the shit from the sewer while dyin' of the clawing gravel and a hardened elephant shit – grotesque, grotesque, grotesque – in the extreme grotesqueness of a gargoyling gargoyle, gargoyle.

Parking Lot Love

Parking lot love with the lovliness filled, sweet mean-ass ramblings (of your DJ Tenderheart) – where the world has a face like Harrison Ford buttfucking the religion-filled neurotic need to die. Delusionally control-pushing lies outta Mel Gibson's eyes!! I create OPEN and reveal the parallel universe of simple night-time romance!
You can't be pretentious when she's 'bout to leave you in a parking lot for you to be judge, jury, 'n witness of your own...

MC Tenderheart! Where the newspapers scream, shout and the waters getting' dirty and the garbage is waiting to get fucked 'n dumped, and purest trash rolls to meet...
What lies inside the darkwinds of you, the night! For you are the night's secrets and you are finally at the end of your own night. For the secrets you finally deem non-with-holdable have become uncontrollably MAAAAAD AAAAAAT YOOOOOOUUUU!!!

Redeem mmmmm... your lotto... eat your quick dog... 'n there she is, ahhhh! 'n now was by the Slurpee machine, and the tar top kisses the bottoms o' your boots and, ignored by you... it tried to tell you!!!

The dirt on yer boots are sweet succulent memories – you – ignored the detail of me!!! Your never-ending road to never finding her!!! Go home! To sleep alone! Again! Someday when you had enough nothin'!!!

As you pick yourself off the parking lot shining blue black flat-top – you will say: "Oh oh the light o' the moon, bounces off the tar! And waits for me to live with love that only lives between moon 'n street! Interfered with all my fear 'n regret never having said you are my parking lot love.

Made in the USA
Lexington, KY
14 December 2016